THE BATTLE OF TINIAN

THE CAPTURE OF THE ATOMIC BOMB ISLAND, JULY – AUGUST 1944

THE BATTLE OF TINIAN

THE CAPTURE OF THE ATOMIC BOMB ISLAND, JULY – AUGUST 1944

John Grehan and Alexander Nicoll

Frontline Books

THE BATTLE OF TINIAN
The Capture of the Atomic Bomb Island, July – August 1944

First published in Great Britain in 2023 by Frontline Books,
an imprint of Pen & Sword Books Ltd,
Yorkshire – Philadelphia

Typeset in 9.5/12.5 Avenir by Dave
Cassan Printed and bound by CPI UK

Pen & Sword Books Ltd incorporates the imprints of Air World Books, After the Battle, Pen & Sword Archaeology, Atlas, Aviation, Battleground, Discovery, Family History, History, Maritime, Military, Naval, Politics, Social History, Transport, True Crime, Claymore Press, Frontline Books, Praetorian Press, Seaforth Publishing and White Owl.

For a complete list of Pen & Sword titles please contact:

PEN & SWORD BOOKS LTD
47 Church Street, Barnsley, South Yorkshire, S70 2AS, UK.
E-mail: enquiries@pen-and-sword.co.uk
Website: www.pen-and-sword.co.uk

Or

PEN AND SWORD BOOKS,
1950 Lawrence Road, Havertown, PA 19083, USA
E-mail: uspen-and-sword@casematepublishers.com
Website: www.penandswordbooks.com

CONTENTS

ACKNOWLEDGEMENTS

The authors and publisher would like to extend their grateful thanks, in no particular order, to the following individuals and organisations for their assistance with the images used in this publication: Robert Mitchell, James Luto, Historic Military Press, US Naval History and Heritage Command, US National Museum of Naval Aviation, US National Archives and Records Administration, National Museum of the US Air Force, United States Air Force, US Navy, US Library of Congress, US Army, the National Museum of the US Navy and the USMC Archives.

Introduction

FORAGING FOR VICTORY

The great wave of success which in nine months carried the Japanese halfway across the Pacific had begun to recede with the loss of Guadalcanal in the first weeks of 1943. During the intervening months, the Allies, led by the USA, had laid a solid foundation for the recovery of their lost territories. Towards the end of that year, the Allies were poised to breach the Japanese inner defensive perimeter, which included the Mariana Islands, Palau, Western New Guinea, and the Dutch East Indies. The Japanese sought to defend this perimeter to the last, but this line was too extensive, and the islands too widely separated by the vast reaches of the Pacific Ocean, to halt the Allies, who struck in November 1943 with landings in the Gilbert Islands.

Below: US Marine Corps LVTs head for the shore as part of the first wave of the US landings on Saipan, 15 June 1944. (USNHHC)

Left: A Douglas SBD Dauntless from USS *Lexington* flies over Tanapag Harbor, Saipan, during the landings on 15 June 1944. (USNHHC)

The isolated garrisons in the Gilberts were overwhelmed, as were the Japanese forces on the Marshall Islands, the latter being finally subdued in early 1944. With their perimeter pierced, the Japanese Imperial General Headquarters looked for an alternative plan. Rather than see their forces picked off one by one, the Japanese decided to concentrate as much of their strength as possible in one final cataclysmic battle. The new plan was given the codename *A-Go*.

For their part, the Allies continued their remorseless advance, with the next objective, the Mariana Islands, squarely in their sights. The Marianas were of profound significance on two levels. The first was that the largest island in the archipelago, Saipan, was not somewhere that had been captured by the Japanese during the war, but was Japanese territory with a large civilian Japanese population. The second was that the islands, which also included Guam and Tinian, were close enough to Tokyo and the Japanese home islands to be within the operational range of the new Boeing B-29 Superfortress four-engine, high-altitude, strategic heavy bomber.

At around $3 billion, the design and development of the B-29 represented the most expensive weapons programme of the Second World War. It had been conceived especially for the Pacific theatre due to the enormous distances that aircraft would have to cover. Though initially deployed in the European theatre, by the end of 1943, the B-29 was dedicated to the Pacific. But what the USAAF required at this stage was a base from which it could operate the Superfortress to bomb Japan into what, it was hoped, would be submission. That base was to be the Marianas.

The Japanese believed that the Americans were likely to make their next move against

the Carolines or the Palaus islands, but on 12 June 1944 strikes by US Navy carrier-borne aircraft on the Marianas convinced them that, in fact, it was those islands which were in danger. As a result, the commander of the Imperial Japanese Navy's Combined Fleet, Admiral Soemu Toyoda, was instructed to prepare to intercept the US ships heading for the Marianas and bring about what was hoped would be the decisive battle, or *Kantai Kessen*, of the war in the Pacific.

OPERATION FORAGER

Exactly three months earlier, on 12 March 1944, the US Joint Chiefs of Staff had issued a directive to Admiral Chester W. Nimitz, Commander-in-Chief Pacific Ocean Areas, to prepare for an invasion of the Mariana Islands. Such a move was scheduled to be launched under the codename Operation *Forager*.

The Northern Marianas consists of fourteen mostly uninhabited islands. Most of their population was found on the three larger islands – namely Saipan, Tinian, and Rota. The largest and southernmost island of the Mariana archipelago is Guam. This, as distinct from the Northern Marianas, had been a US territory before its capture by the Japanese in 1941. By the summer of 1944, the Marianas had become the base of the Japanese Central Pacific Fleet under Admiral Nagumo Chuichi and the 31st Army under Lieutenant General Hideyoshi Obata, though command of the Japanese forces on Saipan was in the hands of Lieutenant General Yoshitsugu Saitō.

The Americans decided that the best course of action was to invade Saipan first, followed by Tinian and Guam. D-Day for the landings on Saipan was set for 15 June 1944.

Left: The USS *New Mexico* firing in support of the landings on Saipan. Another battleship, USS *Pennsylvania*, can be seen in the background. Note that the middle gun in *New Mexico*'s No.3 turret is in the recoil position. (USNHHC)

Above: US Marines of the first wave ashore on Saipan hug the beach and prepare to move inland on D-Day, 15 June 1944. An LVT, hit by Japanese fire, can be seen burning in the background. (NARA)

Opposite page top: A marine throws a hand grenade at an enemy position on Saipan. A second Marine is about to throw his grenade, the fuze of which is already burning. (USNHHC)

Opposite page bottom: US Marines, advancing in rugged terrain, clearing the enemy from the caves on Saipan during the fighting in June 1944. (NARA)

A preliminary bombardment of the Japanese defensive positions on Saipan opened on 13 June, in the course of which a massive weight of shells from the American battleships, cruisers and destroyers rained down on the island. Then, as planned, at 07.00 hours on the morning of 15 June, the leading Marines of V Amphibious Corps were carried ashore by amphibious tractors, in the process of which they encountered heavier than expected opposition from the enemy. Intelligence reports had underestimated enemy troop levels which, being in excess of 31,000 men, were as much as double the forecasts and, for at least a month, Japanese forces had been fortifying the island and bolstering its forces.

The American casualties on D-Day were high, with as many as 3,500 men being hit in the first twenty-four hours of the invasion. Despite this, by sunset on that first day, 20,000 men were ashore, with many more to come. The unexpectedly heavy resistance was not the only concern of the Fifth Fleet commander Admiral Raymond Spruance. For as well as providing naval and air support for the landings, he had to watch for Toyoda's Combined Fleet, which was known to be on the move.

Main image: One of the most iconic images of the Battle of Saipan, this photograph shows US troops stumbling after being hit by Japanese fire during the landings to the south of Garapan. (NARA)

'The [Japanese] are coming after us,' Spruance declared. That enemy force was formidable, amounting to five battleships, eleven heavy cruisers, two light cruisers, some twenty-eight destroyers and nine aircraft carriers with almost 500 aircraft. The day of the *Kantai Kessen* was approaching.[1]

THE BATTLE OF THE PHILIPPINE SEA

Impressive as Toyoda's armada may seem, it was in fact overshadowed by the might of the ships and aircraft that sailed with Vice Admiral Marc Mitscher's Task Force 58 to confront the Combined Fleet. Mitscher could boast fifteen carriers, carrying between them some 905 fighters, torpedo bombers and dive bombers. They would be unleashed against an enemy who had been unable to replace many of its experienced aircrew following the heavy losses the Japanese had incurred at the battles of the Coral Sea and Midway. As well as understanding that the impending battle would be the most decisive of the war against America, many Japanese knew that it was also likely to be their last.

What became known as the Battle of the Philippine Sea opened between the two great naval forces on 19 June. Although both sides sent aircraft to locate opposing fleets, the Japanese found the Americans and struck first. Admiral Jisaburō Ozawa sent forty-three aircraft out on a scouting mission, with one pilot spotting and reporting the location of Mitscher's task force 160 miles west of Saipan.

Throughout the day, Ozawa's fighters and bombers attacked Task Force 58 in four successive waves but were shattered by the more experienced American fighters flying protection for the carriers. Ozawa had expected to be supported by land-based aircraft but raids by the Americans that same day against Japanese airfields on Guam, Saipan, and Tinian meant there were far fewer aircraft to help him than he had envisaged. The result for the Americans was a two-to-one advantage in airpower – it was a devastating outcome for the Japanese pilots and aircrew.

It was not until the afternoon of the following day, 20 June, that Ozawa's fleet was located. However, the reported position placed the Japanese ships 275 miles away, far beyond the safe limit of Mitscher's bombers. Nevertheless, he did not hesitate to attack, even though a second report showed that the Japanese were, in fact, steaming even further away.

As evening began to fall on 20 June, a force of 216 Helldivers, Avengers, and Hellcats attacked Ozawa's fleet. With only seventy-five aircraft left to protect his ships, Ozawa looked on powerlessly as first one carrier was sunk and then three others heavily damaged. Twenty US aircraft were destroyed in the attack by anti-aircraft fire, while sixty-five of the seventy-five Japanese fighters were shot down.

Mitscher's airmen had all but wrecked Ozawa's carrier force, but they then faced the prospect of trying to find their ships in the growing darkness with their fuel gauges alarmingly low. Though Mitscher ordered his carriers to turn on all their lights, despite the danger of them being spotted

Opposite page top: Seen from USS *Monterey*, the carrier USS *Bunker Hill* just narrowly misses being hit by a Japanese bomb during the Battle of the Philippine Sea, 19 June 1944. The Japanese aircraft, its tail shot off, can be seen crashing on the far left. (USNHHC)

Opposite page bottom: As the Battle of the Philippine Sea unfolds, the Japanese aircraft carrier *Zuikaku*, in the centre surrounded by bomb bursts, and two destroyers are pictured here manoeuvring while under attack by US Navy carrier aircraft during the late afternoon of 20 June 1944. *Zuikaku* was hit by several bombs during these attacks but survived. (USNHHC)

by enemy submarines, many aircraft failed to return, while others were forced to ditch into the sea when they ran out of fuel.

What is regarded as the greatest carrier battle of the war ended with the almost complete elimination of Japan's naval air power. For the loss of 123 aircraft and 109 dead, the US Navy had destroyed nearly 600 enemy aircraft, sank two enemy fleet carriers, a light carrier, and two oilers. In the process, some 3,000 of the IJN's pilots and sailors were killed. Nothing now could prevent the Allies from completing Operation *Forager*, though it would take them far longer than anticipated.

SUICIDE NOT SURRENDER

It took six days for the US Marines to fully secure their beachhead on the south-west coast of Saipan. The next step for Lieutenant General Holland M. Smith's men was to pursue the Japanese who had withdrawn into the hills in the centre of the island. The attack upon the enemy positions on Mount Tipo Pale and Mount Tapochau began on 22 June, with the US Army's 27th Division having landed to support the Marines.

As expected, the advance was slow and deadly, the features of the ground labelled by the Americans as 'Death Valley' and 'Purple Heart Ridge' starkly portraying the savagery of the combat. Gradually, though, the Japanese were driven back until they were squeezed into their last positions on the northern extremity of the island.

With defeat an inevitability, General Saitō threw his men at the invaders in a final, but futile, banzai charge. He ordered his bedraggled band to *Gyokusai* – die with honour. Having instructed his men to head to their deaths, Saitō then took his own life.

At 04.45 hours on 7 July, just as daylight began to pierce the early morning sky, the sound of bugles echoed across the Tanapag Plain on Saipan. Moments later, a rag-tag army of thousands of Japanese soldiers, sailors, and, according to one witness, civilian construction workers, armed with rifles, spears, or just their bare hands, charged, hobbled or limped towards the American lines, yelling and screaming as they did so.

Swarming down the valleys and onto the narrow coastal plain, they found a gap between the 1st and 2nd battalions of the US 105th Infantry and ran on towards the regimental headquarters. The Japanese may have been little more than a disorganized rabble, but Major Hoffman USMC later recalled that, 'Here was a determination which was seldom – if ever – matched by fighting men of any other country'.[2]

'All hell broke loose,' remembered Lieutenant George O'Donnell of Company G of the 105th's 2nd Battalion, as the Americans were gradually forced back, in some cases into the streets of the town of Tanapag itself. 'From our right and below us, there came thousands of Japs! For two hours they passed by, and came right at us. It was like a mob after a big football game, all trying to get out at once! We had a hard struggle keeping them from overrunning us, and had a field day, firing, firing until our ammunition started to run low. The closest any of them came was ten yards, and we were hitting them at four hundred and five hundred yards also.'[3]

The Japanese were slaughtered as they threw themselves at the 105th and the US Marine Corps artillery, which fired at will over open sights at virtually point-blank range. The bodies of the attackers became piled so high in front of the guns, the Marines had to move round them to retain an open

Left: Japanese prisoners are brought in from their isolated positions on Saipan during mopping up operations, 4 July 1944. (NARA)

Above: A view taken from the beach near Tanapag, on Saipan's north-west coast, of part of the area in which the banzai charge was made on 7 July 1944. The attack was launched from the high ground in the distance, an area that was later termed Harakiri Gulch. (John Grehan Collection)

Opposite page: During the mass suicides which took place on Saipan at the end of the American operation there, many individuals, soldiers and civilians alike, threw themselves into the sea at what today is called Banzai Cliff. (John Grehan Collection)

field of fire – and still the Japanese kept coming. The infantry and Marines hung on into the afternoon, despite heavy losses, when, at last, the 106th Regiment came to their help.

Among the relentless Japanese attackers was Mitsuharu Noda. 'We were ordered there to be killed,' Noda once remarked. 'Some probably may have got drunk, just to overcome fear … It was a kind of suicide … We hardly had any arms. Some only had shovels, others had sticks. I had a pistol. I think I was shot at the second line of defence. Hit by two bullets in my stomach, one passing through, one lodging in me … I woke up when [the Americans] kicked me and they took me to the field hospital.'

Noda was, unquestionably, one of the lucky ones, for the events that followed the *Gyokusai* were almost too horrible to witness. The Tanapag Plain was strewn with the bodies of the fallen Japanese – 4,311 according to one source[4]. With little option, they were ploughed into mass graves by bulldozers. The 105th suffered almost 1,000 casualties.

Above: The battered shell of General Saito's and Vice Admiral Nagumo's last command post at Marpi Point at the northern tip of Saipan. (John Grehan Collection)

Not all the Japanese had taken part in the charge, with some men, as well as civilians, found to be still holding out in the cliffs of the island's most northerly peninsular, Marpi Point. With no possibility of escape, most of those individuals killed themselves, and often their families, many throwing themselves to their deaths from what will always be known as Suicide Cliff.

Saipan was declared secure on 9 July 1944. There was to be little respite for the two US Marine Corps divisions, however, as they were immediately earmarked for the invasion of Tinian, which was to begin on 24 July.

Meanwhile, the men of III Amphibious Corps had launched their assault upon Guam. In the original US plan, Guam was to be assaulted three days after the landings on Saipan. But so dogged had been Saitō's defence, the attack had to be postponed. It was not until 21 July that Lieutenant General Holland M. Smith was ready to launch the invasion of this island.

Above: US Marines take cover on one of the landing beaches during the initial landings on Guam, 21 July 1944. (NARA)

Guam had been shelled along with Saipan during the preliminary bombardment on 12 June, and then attacked from the air on 19 July. Nevertheless, its well-prepared defences were subjected to further naval and air strikes ahead of, and during, the amphibious assault which was delivered either side of the Orote Peninsular with its airfield and adjacent harbour on the island's western coast.

Lieutenant General Obata had the 19,000 men of the Japanese 31st Army under his command. As Saitō had done on Saipan, Obata planned to try and halt the Americans on the landing beaches where they would be at their most vulnerable. But should the invaders manage to gain a solid foothold, Obata would withdraw to the hills and fight it out there to the bitter end.

The fighting on the beaches was desperate, and the first night ashore a long one for the 3rd Marine Division and the 77th Infantry Division. Beating off savage counter-attacks, the Americans hung on and, as more troops were landed, they were able to push inland and, on 28 July, the two

beachheads were joined. There was no longer any point in the Japanese trying to hold the Americans on the coast, and Obata fell back to the mountains in the centre and north of the island.

The island's capital was liberated on 31 July, as the Marines and the infantry began their final push. Obata prepared for his last stand on the Mount Santa Rosa on the north-eastern coast. The Japanese positions were pounded by the American artillery and then stormed by the 77th Division. The last few Japanese were wiped out on the beach below the heights. Though a small number of Obata's men held out in the jungle for a further twelve months, all organized resistance in Guam ended on 10 August 1944.

Left: The battleship USS *New Mexico* is pictured during its preparations for landings on Guam in July 1944. Rows of 14-inch projectiles can be seen on the starboard side of the battleship's deck as the crew replenish her ammunition supply. Note the triple 14/50 gun turrets on the left. (USNHHC)

Above: The scene on Asan Beach, on the western coast of Guam, as seen one hour and a half after the first landings on July 21 1944. With LVTs and M-4 Sherman tanks beyond, a field dressing station can be seen in operation in the foreground. (NARA)

Overleaf: Mindful of the risk of snipers, US Marines enter the ruins of Guam's capital, Agana, today known as Hagåtña, on 31 July 1944. (USNHHC)

TINIAN TIMELINE

1944

11 June	Task Force 58 begins bombardment of Tinian and Saipan.
14 June	Fire support ships of the Northern and Southern Attack Forces commence bombardment of Saipan and Tinian.
15 June	2nd and 4th Marine divisions land at Saipan.
16 June	27th Infantry Division begins landing at Saipan.
	Bombardment of Guam by surface ships commences.
19-20 June	Battle of the Philippine Sea. Japanese Imperial Navy suffers decisive defeat.
20 June	Battery B, 531st Field Artillery Battalion, XXIV Corps Artillery, commences fires on Tinian from positions on Saipan.
21 June	Aslito airfield on Saipan becomes operational for US fighter aircraft.
24 June	The whole of the 531st Field Artillery Battalion commences firing on Tinian from positions on Saipan.
26 June	Admiral Turner issues new plan for intensification of Tinian bombardment.
6-7 July	Japanese personnel launch a savage banzai attack along Tanapag Plain on Saipan.
9 July	4th Marine Division reaches Marpi Point; Saipan declared secured; mop-up begins.
10 July	2nd and 4th Marine divisions prepare for Tinian operation.
10-11 July	Amphibious Reconnaissance Battalion, V Amphibious Corps, and Underwater Demolition Team 5 reconnoitre the Tinian landing beaches.
13 July	Northern Troops and Landing Force issues Tinian Operation Order.
15 July	Rear Admiral Harry W. Hill assumes command of the Northern Attack Force, relieving Vice Admiral Richmond K. Turner.
18 July	The Japanese Prime Minister, Hideki Tōjō, and his Cabinet resign.
20 July	First troops for Tinian invasion embark aboard ships at Saipan.
21 July	Southern Troops and Landing Force lands on Guam.
24 July	The US 4th Marine Division lands on Tinian.

24-25 July	Japanese launch powerful night counter-attacks against 4th Marine Division beachhead and suffer decisive defeat.
25 July	2nd Marine Division completes its landing on Tinian.
27 July	Ushi Point Airfield, Tinian, becomes operational for US aircraft.
30 July	Tinian town captured.
31 July	At 02.00 hours, Japanese counter-attack strikes the 1st and 2nd battalions, 8th Marines, on Tinian.
1 August	All organized resistance ceases on Tinian; island declared secured.
3 August	At 15.00 hours, the United States' flag is officially raised over Tinian.
9 August	Aslito airfield, Saipan, becomes operational for Consolidated B-24 bombers.
10 August	Organized resistance ends on Guam and the island is declared secured.
15 October	Aslito airfield, Saipan, becomes operational for B-29s.
24 November	Saipan-based B-29s raid Tokyo.
30 December	B-29s land at Tinian.

1945

4 February	Tinian-based B-29s raid the Kobe area, Japan.
16 July	USS *Indianapolis* departs San Francisco with enriched uranium and other parts required for the assembly of the atomic bomb codenamed 'Little Boy'.
26 July	USS *Indianapolis* arrives at Tinian.
30 July	After leaving Tinian, USS *Indianapolis* is sunk en route to Leyte by Japanese submarine *I-58*.
6 August	The Atomic bomb 'Little Boy', carried by Tinian-based B-29, is dropped on Hiroshima.
9 August	A second atomic bomb carried from Tinian is dropped on Nagasaki.
10 August	Japan sues for peace.

NORTHERN MARIANA ISLANDS
(UNITED STATES)

Farallon
de Pajaros

Maug
Islands

Asuncion

*NORTH
PACIFIC
OCEAN*

Agrihan

Pagan

N o r t h e r n   M a r i a n a   I s l a n d s

Alamagan

Guguan

*PHILIPPINE
SEA*

Sarigan

Anatahan

Farallon de
Medinilla

Saipan Saipan

Tinian

Aguijan

Rota
reef

*NORTH
PACIFIC
OCEAN*

The Northern Mariana Islands,
with Tinian just to the south
of the islands' current capital,
Saipan. (Shutterstock)

**Hagåtña
(Agana)**
reef Guam
(U.S.)

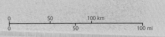

| 0 | | 50 | | 100 km |
| 0 | | 50 | | 100 mi |

Chapter 1

PLANS AND PREPARATIONS

3 June 1942

The island of Tinian is located around 1,250 nautical miles to the south-east of Tokyo and, along with Saipan, formed the Japanese defence area of the Marianas. The two islands are, though, physically quite different. Unlike the rugged, mountainous terrain of Saipan, Tinian is generally open and flat. This made it ideal for the construction of airfields, with the result that the Japanese built two on the island, one of which, with a 4,750-foot runway at Ushi Point, was more than 1,000 feet longer than Aslito airfield on Saipan.

Below: A periscope photograph of the Sunharon refinery and oil tanks on Tinian that was taken by USS *Flying Fish* during her reconnaissance of the Marianas in early February 1943. (USNHHC)

Above: An American air attack against Japanese shipping at Tinian underway on 23 February 1944. This raid was made in conjunction with strikes against targets on Saipan. (NARA)

In 1944, Tinian was largely taken over with sugar cane fields interspersed with the occasional grove of trees. From its sharp Ushi Point in the north to its blunt Lalo Point in the south, the island is approximately 12.25 miles long. At its widest point, near the centre of the island, Tinian measures just under six miles. However, apart from the area around Tinian Harbor on the south-west coast, adjacent to what was called Tinian Town and is now known as San Jose, the island is almost entirely encircled by cliffs which rise perpendicularly from the sea as much as 100 feet, rendering any amphibious assault impracticable.

Only two other spots, marked by sandy beaches and breaks in the cliffs, were likely landing places. One of these is at the north-west of the island, where there are two short beaches, one sixty yards wide, the other around 160 yards wide. These, though, are separated by nearly 1,000 yards of 'tortuous' coral outcropping. About 100 yards out from the beaches was a coral reef shelf, which meant that the beaches could only be used for landing infantry. On the east coast, again, are two short beaches, each no more than 125 yards wide. Only one of these had been identified by US intelligence as being 'suitable for spot landings'.

The Japanese garrison on Tinian consisted primarily of Colonel Kiyochi Ogata's 50th Infantry Regiment which, with supporting detachments, numbered 5,052 men. There was also a small naval force under the command of Captain Goichi Oya. Also present was Vice Admiral Kakuji Kakuda,

Above: Smoke rises from the runway of a Japanese airfield on Tinian after a US air raid on 23 February 1944. (NARA)

whose 1st Air Fleet Headquarters (about 200 men) was based on Tinian. Almost all of his aircraft had been lost at the Battle of the Philippine Sea or destroyed by the US air raids.

As the Americans closed in on Tinian, Kakuta and his staff made repeated efforts to escape in rubber boats at prearranged rendezvous points with a Japanese submarine. After several failed attempts, they withdrew to a cave on the east coast of Tinian and the admiral was never seen again. It is presumed that he committed suicide.

Exclusive of Kakuta's headquarters, the remaining naval contingent numbered 3,910, giving Ogata just under 9,000 men to defend the island. Included in that figure was Lieutenant Shikamura's Tank Company of the 18th Infantry Regiment with twelve light tanks, as well as one 75mm mountain artillery unit, of three four-gun batteries, and one anti-tank platoon with six 37mm guns. While Captain Oya was supposed to be under Ogata's orders, he acted independently, making his own preparations for the attack everyone on the island knew was coming. It should be mentioned that there were also three civilian defence organisations, but these had been issued with little in the way of weapons, aside from a stash of hand grenades with which to blow up themselves and their families to avoid capture.

Ogata did not regard the north-western beaches as likely landing points, assuming instead that the Americans would probably land along the beaches facing Tinian Town or on the two east coast beaches between Asiga Point and Masalog Point. Consequently, he placed just one of his battalions in the north of the island to defend Ushi Point airfield and another battalion in the south around Tinian Town. He held another battalion in the south-centre of the island as a mobile reserve which, along with the Tank Company, was to 'advance rapidly to the place of landings, depending on the situation, and attack'. His fourth battalion was in reserve and dug-in on the island's highest point, the 561-foot Mount Lasso, in the centre of the island to the north of Tinian Town.

Ogata's defensive plan differed little from those of Saitō on Saipan and Obata on Guam. He told his unit commanders to be ready to 'counterattack to the water and ... destroy the enemy on beaches with one blow ... But in the eventuality we have been unable to expel the enemy ... we will gradually fall back on our prepared positions ... and defend them to the last man.'[5]

The operational body created to capture Saipan and Tinian was designated the Northern Troops and Landing Force (NTLF), and constituted the 2nd and 4th Marine divisions, commanded by Major General Thomas E. Watson and Major General Harry Schmidt respectively. The United States' complete mastery of the skies over Tinian allowed numerous reconnaissance flights to be undertaken, enabling NTLF's officers to undertake detailed and precise planning. What they saw was encouraging: 'The roads were all North-South and East-West and that the sugar cane fields were layed [sic] out in square blocks, again N-S and E-W. It was observed likewise that tree plantings, grown as wind breaks for the sugar cane, fringed the fields in the same N-S-E-W plan. This regular pattern ... permitted a remarkably simple series of boundaries for the control of uniform advances by our troops.'[6]

As the north-western beaches appeared to be undefended these became the focus of the NTLF commanders; they were duly designated 'White 1' and 'White 2' beaches. However, due to their extreme narrowness, considerable doubts remained whether large bodies of Marines or troops could be landed there, and questions were raised about how practicable it would be to keep the invaders reinforced and supplied.

Left: An aerial view of Magicienne Bay (foreground) and Aslito Field (middle distance) on Saipan that was taken on 29 May 1944. Part of the island of Tinian can be seen in the background. (USNHHC)

Above: US Navy warships at Majuro, the capital and largest city of the Marshall Islands, on 5 June 1944, just before their departure for the Marianas. Many of these ships are from Task Force 58, and include the four battleships on the right, these being USS *Iowa*, USS *New Jersey*, USS *North Carolina*, and USS *Washington*.

These concerns had to be addressed before the assault could be considered. So, the Amphibious Reconnaissance Battalion, V Amphibious Corps and Underwater Demolition Team 5 conducted a secret physical reconnaissance of the White beaches and the stretch of the east coast between Asiga and Masalog Points, which was designated 'Yellow Beach'.

The report of the reconnaissance parties indicated that White 1 and White 2 beaches both offered extremely restricted landing areas for vehicles. That said, it was found that waterproofed vehicles could safely clear the reef, while the cliffs which flanked the beaches were low enough for the troops to climb over. The reconnaissance missions also suggested that there were no mines or any other man-made obstacles on both White beaches. This was not the case with Yellow Beach, where underwater obstacles, mines, barbed wire and almost insurmountable cliffs were encountered, as well as evidence of ongoing construction of fortifications immediately inland.

Major General Harry Schmidt, who had led the 4th Marine Division at Saipan,[7] took command of the force designated for Tinian – V Amphibious Corps – on 12 July and he quickly concluded that the landing would take place on the White beaches. Among the reasons he advanced, apart from the obvious element of surprise that would be achieved by landing in the north and the opposition that would be encountered at Tinian Town and on Yellow Beach, was that landing close to Ushi Point airfield meant that it could be captured quickly and then be used for resupply – thus overcoming one of the main concerns with landing on the White beaches.

This met with the approval of the operation's naval staff. 'The more we looked at the Tinian Town beaches, the less we liked them,' remarked Rear Admiral Harry W. Hill. 'My staff was of one mind: land on the northern end of the island.' Schmidt issued his orders the following day.

The 4th Marine Division was to land on White 1 and White 2 beaches on what was termed 'Jig-Day', or J-Day. From there they would push inland to capture the low Mount Maga, which sits a short distance inland from the beaches, and then move on to take Mount Lasso and Asiga Point on the east. To deceive the enemy into believing that the attack would be delivered against Tinian Town, the 2nd Marine Division would appear off Tinian Harbor, along with a sizeable naval force, until the 4th Division had landed on the two White beaches. This force would then sail north to follow and support the 4th Division.

A further advantage offered by the use of these northern beaches was that artillery positioned on the south-western coast of Saipan would be able to reach that area of Tinian, and so could fire in support of the landing. The plans dictated that four batteries of XXIV Corps Artillery would deliver indirect fire onto any enemy positions that might stand in the path of the Marines. The 27th Infantry Division on Saipan would act as the reserve, ready to embark on landing craft at four hours' notice.

Schmidt had more than 40,000 men under his immediate command and could call on many more from the army's 27th Division, let alone powerful artillery and naval support. There could only be one result to the Battle of Tinian.

However, Schmidt's Marines had suffered heavy casualties in the fighting so far (around 10,500 on Saipan alone) and there was no knowing how long the war was to last and what might be expected of the men in the months to come. The tenacious and even suicidal methods employed by the Japanese on Saipan were likely to be repeated on Tinian. Lieutenant General Holland M. Smith desperately hoped to avoid the protracted and deadly operations so far experienced in the Marianas. So, if the Marines could quickly take Mount Lasso before the main Japanese body retreated into the high ground, there was a good chance of eliminating the enemy both rapidly and with comparatively little loss. Speed and surprise would be essential.

Major General Clifton B. Cates took over command of the 4th Marine Division, to which the tanks of the 2nd Marine Division were attached to give the assault a more powerful 'punch'. For the initial assault, the 4th Division's 2nd Marine Regiment was to land on White 2 and the 8th Marines was to land on White 1, with the 6th Marines following behind ready to land on either beach. The problem of supply over the narrow beaches was to be overcome as far as possible by moving supplies by trucks and tractors straight to the divisional ready dumps instead of the usual method of manhandling materials onto stockpiles on the beaches. For this, eighty-eight cargo trucks and twenty-five trailers would move the supplies from twenty LCTs (Landing Craft, Tank) and ten LCMs (Landing Craft, Mechanized).

Overleaf: Supplies are pictured being loaded aboard transports, including LSTs, at Saipan in preparation for the assault on Tinian, July 1944. (USNHHC)

Still concerned with the narrowness of the beaches, thought was given to finding a means of extending the length of the landing area for vehicles, and the planners came up with an ingenious idea of providing access over the low cliffs that flanked the beaches. Engineers devised portable ramps, each of which would be supported by two steel beams.

The whole assembly could be carried by LVTs.[8] When they reached the foot of the cliffs the ramp would be laid at an angle of 45 degrees over the cliff, enabling vehicles up to the weight of a thirty-five-ton tank to pass along the ramp, the deck of which was constructed from eighteen thick wooden planks. Arrangements were also made to re-supply the Marines by air drops and as soon as Ushi Point airfield was in US hands, aircraft from Saipan would be able to fly in 100 tons a day.

With Tinian's west coast exposed to the region's prevailing winds, Admiral Hill had insisted that he needed three days of calm weather to ensure a successful landing. With favourable forecasts received on 20 July, Admiral Spruance, Commander Fifth Fleet, confirmed that J-Day would be 24 July. What was termed 'How-Hour' was set for 07.30 hours.

That same day, 20 July, with the plans all laid and the first the troops beginning to embark at Saipan for the invasion of Tinian, Admiral Turner and Holland Smith could then turn their attention to Guam, which was about to be attacked on the 21st. Before departing for Guam, Turner said to General Schmidt: 'I'll give you two weeks to take Tinian.'

'Admiral,' Schmidt replied, 'we will take that place in ten days'.

Chapter 2

BOMBARDMENT

11 June–23 July 1944

Tinian was to be subjected to a massive land, air and sea bombardment ahead of the landings. In fact, the island first came under attack as early as 11 June 1944, when Operation *Forager* began, and Tinian had continued to be targeted both day and night. But from 22 July, two days ahead of the landings, the bombardment was to be intensified.

Targets in the northern half of the island were to be the responsibility of the Saipan-based artillery, while those in the south handed to the Navy. Any objectives or locations that could not be

Below: Grumman TBM Avenger bombers prepare to take off from the Independence-class light aircraft carrier USS *Monterey* to attack enemy positions on Tinian, June 1944. (US Navy)

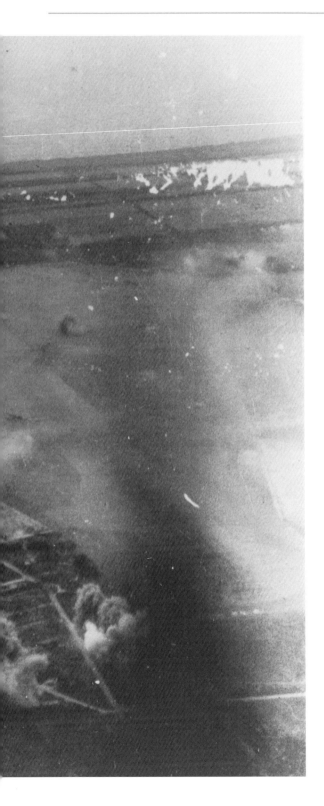

satisfactorily reached by either land or naval artillery would be left to the aircraft of Mitscher's Task Force 58 and USAAF aircraft flying from Aslito airfield. Included in the aerial bombardment would be a new weapon – the napalm bomb.

This new development in aerial warfare was invented by USAAF personnel at Eglin Air Force Base in Florida in early 1944. 'The ingredients were,' notes the historian Richard Harwood, 'diesel oil, gasoline, and a metallic salt from the naptha [sic] used in the manufacture of soap. Mixed with petroleum fuels, the salt created an incendiary jelly that clung to any surface and burned with an extremely hot flame. The concoction was called "napalm." It could be dropped in wing or belly tanks attached to the underside of an aircraft and was fired by an igniter on contact with the ground.'

On 19 July, five days before the Tinian landings, Lieutenant Commander Louis W. Wang, USN arrived at Saipan. He brought with him a small supply of the 'napalm' powder and a demonstration film made at Eglin. Depicting P-47s making low-level drops after diving from 2,000 feet, it vividly demonstrated the potency of the new bombs.

'The demonstration film so impressed Admiral Harry Hill and Major General Harry Schmidt,' continued Harwood, 'that Hill immediately radioed Admiral Chester Nimitz in Hawaii, requesting 8,599 pounds of the powder. They also ordered trial raids on Tinian by P-47 pilots of the Army's 318th Air Group, using powder and detonators already on hand. These trials were not particularly impressive. Their purpose was to burn off wooded areas that had previously resisted white phosphorous and thermite. The "napalm" scorched the trees but left the foliage only

Left: Bombs burst on the Japanese airfield at Tinian as US aircraft make their presence felt on 12 June 1944. (NARA)

13

partially burned. One problem was the wood itself – a virtually indestructible type of ironwood. Another was the napalm mixture. Wang had brought with him the wrong formula. "We tried using Jap aviation gasoline," according to Colonel Lewis M. Sanders, commander of the fighter group, "but that gave too much fire effect. Then we tried Jap motor gas and oil, with the napalm powder, and it was quite successful."[19]

During the two weeks from 26 June to 9 July, the cruisers USS *Indianapolis*, USS *Birmingham* and USS *Montpelier* shelled Tinian on a daily basis. The trio was supplemented in the week preceding Jig-Day by other warships, including *Colorado*, *Tennessee*, and *California*, the cruisers *Louisville*, *Cleveland*, and *New Orleans*, sixteen destroyers, and dozens of supporting vessels. The latter, in particular, fired a variety of ordnance ranging from white phosphorous, which was aimed at wooded areas around the Japanese command post on Mount Lasso, to 40mm fire and rocket barrages by LCIs (Landing Craft, Infantry) directed at caves and other close-in targets.

At 09.00 hours on 22 July, the heavy cruiser USS *New Orleans* opened fire on Tinian with its primary and secondary armament. She continued her bombardment until nightfall. The following morning, on Jig-Day-1, Rear Admiral Harry W. Hill divided the targets on Tinian into five zones which covered the whole of the small island's coastline. Tinian would be shelled from every point on the compass.

With deception deemed more important than destruction, opposite White 1 and White 2 beaches only one ship, the heavy cruiser USS

Right: Battleships and cruisers of Task Force 52 manoeuvre off Saipan and Tinian during the pre-invasion bombardment circa 14 June 1944. This image was taken by the crew of an aircraft operating from USS *Lexington*. The battleship on the right is USS *Pennsylvania*. (USNHHC)

Above: A pall of smoke rises hangs over Tinian Town during a US air strike undertaken in early June 1944. The attackers on this occasion were carrier aircraft from TF-58. This picture was taken by the crew of a 'plane operating from USS *Wasp*. (USNHHC)

Opposite page: The scene in the pilots' ready room of USS *Monterey* as word is awaited from bombers attacking Tinian on 11 June 1944. Among those present are several fighter pilots who have just returned from an earlier strike on the Japanese airfield at Gurguan Point. They included the carrier's Air Group Commander, Lieutenant Commander Roger W. Mehle (seated, right front). To Mehle's right is *Monterey*'s commander, Captain Stuart H. Ingersoll. (NARA)

Louisville, undertook any shelling of the area to suggest that this part of the island was not the Americans' primary objective. Much greater attention was focussed on Tinian Town and the higher ground behind. As part of this, the battleship USS *Colorado*, the light cruiser USS *Cleveland* and four destroyers laid down heavy fire to deceive the Japanese and to cause as much damage and casualties to the enemy and his installations as possible.

In the afternoon, *Colorado* transferred north to join *New Orleans* and five destroyers off the two White beaches and along the north-east coast to fire on the rear of the beaches. Two other battleships, USS *Tennessee* and USS *California*, supported by three destroyers, shelled Yellow Beach, with the battleships also pounding Japanese positions in and around Tinian Town from the rear.

Above: Lieutenant Commander Roger W. Mehle describes the results of an air strike on Tinian to Captain Stuart H. Ingersoll in one of *Monterey's* ready rooms on 11 June 1944. Note Mehle's shoulder holster and revolver. (US Navy)

Right: Elements of the Fire Support Group commanded by Rear Admiral W.L. Ainsworth, TG 52.10, pictured en route to Saipan and Tinian after departing Roi Island, circa 12 June 1944. Photographed from USS *Honolulu*, the various ships are, left to right, *St. Louis*, *Wichita*, *Minneapolis*, *San Francisco*, *New Orleans*, *Idaho*, *Pennsylvania*, *New Mexico* and a pair of escort carriers. (USNHHC)

To avoid the risk of friendly fire accidents, the warships paused at three designated periods during Jig-1 to allow aircraft to fly in low over the island to strike their targets. These struck at junctions on the island's small railway network, as well as observed artillery emplacements, pillboxes and bunkers, plus the beach area in Tinian Town. More than 350 Navy and Army aircraft participated in these strikes, between them dropping some 500 bombs, 200 rockets, forty-two incendiary clusters, and

thirty-four napalm bombs (the latter being carried by USAAF Republic P-47 Thunderbolts). This was only the second use of napalm during the Pacific War; napalm bombs were first used on Tinian just the day before.[10]

The artillery of XXIV Corps, strengthened by the heavier of the two Marine divisions' guns and the 27th Infantry Division, maintained the most consistent of the bombardments, delivering a 'deluge' of shells from Saipan onto the unfortunate island.

By nightfall on 23 July, Tinian was cloaked in thick, black smoke from the explosions of the bombs and shells and the fires of buildings, trees, and cane fields. It must have been all too clear to the defenders that soon – very soon – they would meet their enemies face to face.

Right: USS *Iowa* fires a salvo from its No.2 16-inch turret during the bombardment of Tinian, 14-15 June 1944. (NARA)

Below: The pounding of Japanese positions on Tinian continues on 14–15 June 1944. Once again, this is a shot of USS *Iowa* unleashing another salvo from her after 16-inch turret during the pre-invasion bombardment. (USNHHC)

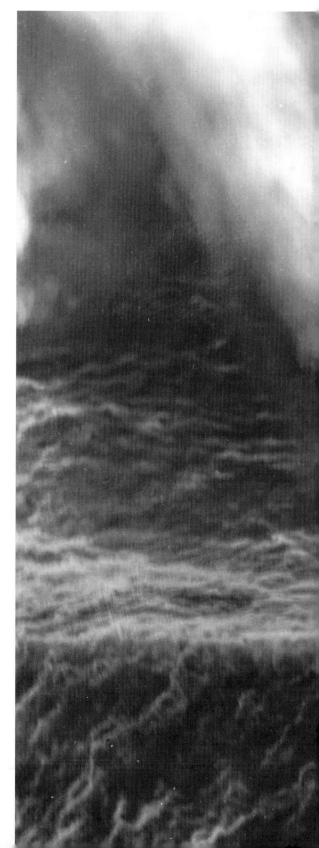

Above: USS *New Orleans* pictured executing a tight turn in Elliot Bay, Washington, on 30 July 1943. She went on to play an integral part in the pre-landing bombardment of Tinian. It was after her preparations for the invasion of the Marianas had been completed in the Marshalls that *New Orleans* sailed from Kwajalein on 10 June 1944. (US Navy)

Below: The cruiser USS *Honolulu* and a destroyer pictured off Tinian on 14 June 1944, as seem from USS *New Mexico*. (USNHHC)

Above: USS *New Jersey* joining in the bombardment of Tinian Island circa 14-15 June 1944. After exercising in the Marshalls for the invasion of the Marianas, *New Jersey* put to sea 6 June in the screening and bombardment group of Admiral Mitscher's Task Force. During the period of the pre-invasion air strikes, *New Jersey* downed an enemy torpedo bomber on 12 June, and during the next two days her heavy guns battered both Saipan and Tinian. (NARA)

Left: USS *New Jersey* fires a salvo one of the 16-inch guns of No.2 turret. Launched in 1942, *New Jersey* saw service in the Korean War before being decommissioned in 1957. In 1968 she was reactivated and outfitted to serve as a heavy bombardment ship in Vietnam. At recommissioning it was the only active battleship in the US Navy. Between late September 1968 and early April 1969, *New Jersey* participated in Operation *Sea Dragon*, providing offshore gunfire support against inland and coastal targets. Soon thereafter, the US Navy decided to reduce heavy bombardment forces in Southeast Asia. USS *New Jersey* was again decommissioned in December 1969. (USNHHC)

Below: Another of the warships that participated in the bombardment of Tinian was the destroyer USS *Fullam*. After training and replenishment at Port Purvis and Espiritu Santo, USS *Fullam* joined the Fifth Fleet for the assault on the Marianas. She arrived off Tinian on 12 June for the bombardments, which began within hours, and continued until the landings. *Fullam* is pictured here refuelling at sea during her service in the Pacific theatre. (USNHHC)

Above: This aerial view of devastated Tinian was taken by a US Navy photographer on 1 July. At the time he was being flown in the US Navy Consolidated B-24 Liberator piloted by Commander Norman M. 'Bus' Miller, USN. Moments before, Miller's crew had dropped their deadly cargo on the target. (US Signal Corps Archive)

Right: An armourer loads 50-calibre machine gun rounds into the ammunition trays on a Republic P-47, that named *Little Rock-ette*, in preparation for a sortie over Tinian, 5 July 1944. (NARA)

Opposite page top: Pilots from the 19th Fighter Squadron, 318th Fighter Group, are debriefed by the squadron's S-2, Lieutenant J.G. Townsend (seen here on the right), at Saipan following their return from an attack on Tinian, 9 July 1944. Note the map and aerial photographs that Townsend is using as part of the process. (NARA)

Opposite page bottom: A controller on one of the airfields on Saipan gives a Republic P-47 Thunderbolt of the 73rd Fighter Squadron, part of the 318th Fighter Group, permission to take-off for sortie to bomb Japanese positions on Tinian, 17 July 1944. (NARA)

Below: Fitted with extra fuel tanks and carrying 500lbs bombs, Republic P-47 Thunderbolts of the 318th Fighter Group take off from Isely Field, Saipan, to attack targets on Tinian, 19 July 1944. Isely Field was constructed following the US capture of Saipan. The original temporary landing field on the site was built by the Japanese Navy in 1933. After it was upgraded following the attack on Pearl Harbor, it was renamed Aslito Field by the Japanese. Under US control, the airfield was further renamed Isely Field in honour of Commander Robert Henry Isely, who was shot down and killed, by anti-aircraft fire, during an attack on Aslito Field on 13 June 1944. At the time, Isely's name was misspelt in official documents and reports as 'Isley', and it was by this incorrect spelling that the airfield was often originally referred. Today, the airfield serves as Saipan's international airport. (NARA)

Above: US Navy personnel on the War Shipping Administration troop transport SS *Dashing Wave* watch from their ship as bombs or shells explode on Tinian, 26 June 1944. (NARA)

Opposite: A napalm bomb explodes on a Japanese position just inland from one of the landing beaches on Tinian. 'In one day,' notes the original caption, 'as much as 10,000 gallons of the liquid fire were dropped from altitudes as low as fifty feet by 7th AAF Thunderbolt fighters on Japanese pillboxes, gun positions, and troop concentrations'. During the fighting on Guam and Tinian, the 318th Fighter Group made much use of 'fire bombs', initially using a mix of diesel and gasoline in drop tanks, before these were replaced by napalm. (NARA)

Below: The busy scene on a US airfield on Saipan, possibly Isely Field once again, as aerial operations continue against Tinian on 19 July 1944. In this view, Republic P-47s of the 19th and 333rd Fighter Squadrons, both part of the 318th Fighter Group, are taxiing into position prior to taking off. (NARA)

Above: A Lockheed P-38 Lightning of the 28th Reconnaissance Squadron, attached to the 318th Fighter Group, comes into land on Saipan following a photographic mission over nearby Tinian on 20 July 1944. (NARA)

Below: The grisly aftermath of the use of 'fire bombs' against Japanese positions on Tinian. The original caption notes that in this instance the 'fire bomb' was dropped on the mouth of an enemy dugout. (NARA)

Above: Another 'fire bomb' dropped by a P-47 Thunderbolt explodes on its target – in this case by part of Tinian's coastline. (NARA)

Below: Vice Admiral Richmond K. Turner, USN, Commander Amphibious Forces Pacific Fleet, peers through captured Japanese binoculars at Tinian Island, which was roughly 2.5 miles away from his vantage point on Saipan, prior to the Marine Corps' landing. Lieutenant General Holland M. Smith, USMC, Commanding General Fleet Marine Force Pacific, can be seen on the right, awaiting his turn at the binoculars. (USNHHC)

Above: The final stages of the pre-landing bombardment of Tinian took place on 24 July – Jig-Day itself – as the invasion forces were making their first moves to capture the island. This image was taken that morning as 'How-Hour' approached. Note the warships in the background. (National Museum of the US Navy)

Chapter 3

JIG-DAY

24 July 1944

As the pre-invasion bombardment entered its last few devastating hours, US Marines, squeezed into the LVTs and the transport ships berthed at Saipan's Tanapag Harbor, shifted around restlessly in attempts to find somewhere comfortable to spend the night. Some preferred to be outside, settling down on the open decks, only to be soaked by passing rain.

Half an hour before sunrise on the morning of 24 July 1944, the armada set off for the brief crossing to the battered island of Tinian. Ahead of it, other warships opened fire on their designated targets, while, above them, aircraft took up their positions to observe the fall of shot and the progress of the assaulting forces or to await confirmation of their targets before launching their own attacks. The gunners on Saipan threw off their exhaustion to increase the tempo even further.

Already, the Demonstration Group was lined up facing the beaches of Tinian Town. USS *Colorado*, USS *Cleveland*, USS *Remey* and USS *Norman Scott* hammered the town and beaches until, a little after 06.00 hours, the seven transport ships carrying the 2nd and 8th regiments of the 2nd Marine Division began lowering their landing craft. The Marines clambered down netting into the landing

Below: A fully-loaded LVT 'churns past a covering warship as it heads for the beach at Tinian' on the morning of Jig-Day, 24 July 1944. (NARA)

craft which then set off for the shore. For all of the world it must have appeared that the Americans were heading straight for the place Colonel Ogata had expected.

Japanese heavy mortars and a well-concealed battery of 6-inch guns engaged the landing craft and the warships, with the big looming structure of USS *Colorado* presenting an unmissable target. The battleship was hit twenty-two times before she moved out of range of the Japanese guns; forty-three men were killed and a further 198 wounded.

When the landing craft were 2,000 yards from the shore they turned round and sped back to the transports. The Japanese in Tinian Town must have believed they had driven off the Americans – but to the north the first elements of the 4th Marines were already motoring towards White 1 and White 2 beaches.

It was at precisely 07.17 hours that the US Marines, loaded into twenty-four LVTs, set off for the twenty-six-minute run to the shore. Ahead of them a number of LCIs, acting as gunboats, raked the beaches with 20mm and 40mm guns and 4.5-inch barrage rockets. At the same time, on either flank battleships, cruisers and destroyers hammered the surrounding areas.

Having encountered only spasmodic rifle and machine-gun fire, the men of Company E of the 24th Marines' 2nd Battalion were the first attackers to land on White 1. At almost the same time, the 25th Marines landed on White 2 with Company A of its 1st Battalion in the lead.

The only opposition encountered at White 1 was where a small number of the enemy were holed up in caves and crevices in the coral cliffs. Embedded in the leading waves was USMC Combat Correspondent Sergeant Gilbert F. Bailey. 'Crouching down low, the Marines ran up over the first small ridge toward the brush,' he recalled. 'A heavier machine gun with a deeper voice started up on the right. They made for the first Jap trench they saw, which wound underground. One of the company cooks jumped in the trench. A cook one day and a rifleman the next.'[11]

For a few minutes the fighting there was intense, but the Japanese were quickly dealt with by the Marines. In less than an hour both battalions of the 24th were ashore and, despite encountering sporadic artillery, mortar, and small arms fire during the first 200 yards of its advance, by nightfall, the regiment reached its first day objective, digging in on the western edge of Ushi Point airfield.

The slightly greater width of White 2 enabled sixteen of the LVTs to land abreast, though half of them were compelled to discharge the Marines onto reefs that flanked the shore. In order to accomplish this, 'two Marines stood at the bow of each LVT and assisted their comrades up to where they could secure a handhold on the jagged coral rim,' recalled Lieutenant Colonel J. Taul. 'Although this method was slow, it did relieve the congestion on the beaches proper and permitted the assault units to advance rapidly inland thus taking full advantage of the surprise gained.'[12]

The Japanese, though, had laid an irregular assortment of anti-personnel mines and booby-traps around the beach. Also blocking the 25th Marines' route were two enemy strongpoints each housing a 47mm gun. Manned by Otaga's 50th Regiment, they had not been destroyed by the preliminary bombardment.

'I will never forget getting out of the landing boat,' remembered Lieutenant Silas 'Moose' Titus of the 25th's Company G. 'And there on the rocks was a shell shocked Jap staring at me with rifle in

Right: A dense column of smoke rises from a Japanese oil dump hit by US Navy warships firing in support of the initial waves of US Marines going ashore on Tinian on Jig-Day. In the foreground, US Coastguard-manned landing craft of the first wave can be seen heading towards the shore. (NARA)

hand; he didn't shoot me so I shot him.'[13] From their well-prepared positions the Japanese poured fire down on the Marines from anti-tank and anti-boat guns, machine-guns, and mortars. These prepared positions were promptly by-passed, to be finally silenced by the following waves as the 25th pushed inland.

With progress proving more rapid on White 1, it was to that beach that the first of the tanks were landed in the form of the 4th Tank Battalion. By 11.00 hours, White 2 was also cleared and ready to receive tanks. Behind the M4 Shermans came the 75mm half-tracks of the weapons companies of the two assault regiments. The first waves of the 4th Division's reserve regiment also began landing at 14.01 hours.

With the 25th also reaching its objective, as darkness crept over the battered little Pacific island on the first day of the invasion, the 4th Marine Division had established a beachhead about 2,900 yards in width and almost a mile deep in the centre. Compared to the bloody and bitter fighting on Saipan, casualties on Tinian had been light, with just 15 killed and 225 wounded.[14]

However, past experience had shown that the first night on such a hostile shore was the most dangerous, with the Japanese likely to mount a counter-attack. So predictable had this response become it was even referred to in a US Army handbook: 'No matter what the situation, a Japanese commander's first reaction to it is to act aggressively to maintain the traditions of his army ... Even when the Japanese commander assumes the defensive, he will, so far as possible, carry out that defense by using the most aggressive tactics that the situation permits.'[15]

Right: Another view of LVTs packed with Marines heading towards the shore on the morning of 24 July 1944. This image was taken by a US Coastguard combat photographer assigned to the Tinian landings. (NARA)

So, having barely stepped ashore, the invaders immediately began taking precautions to counter such a threat. Barbed-wire was strung along the entire length of the division's front, while machine-guns were emplaced with inter-locking fields of fire. At the same time, pack howitzers which had been carried ashore were registered onto points along the main road from Ushi Point airfield and other likely routes of a Japanese advance. The Marines were resupplied with ammunition as they waited for the inevitable pre-dawn attack.

If the Japanese came, the Americans would be ready for them.

Left: The final moments of the run in to shore for one group of LVTs is captured in this photograph taken on 24 July 1944. (USNHHC)

Below: Taken from a distance of four miles, this view of Tinian shows the Japanese defenders under attack on 24 July 1944. The explosions of bombs 'sends up clouds of heavy black smoke'. (NARA)

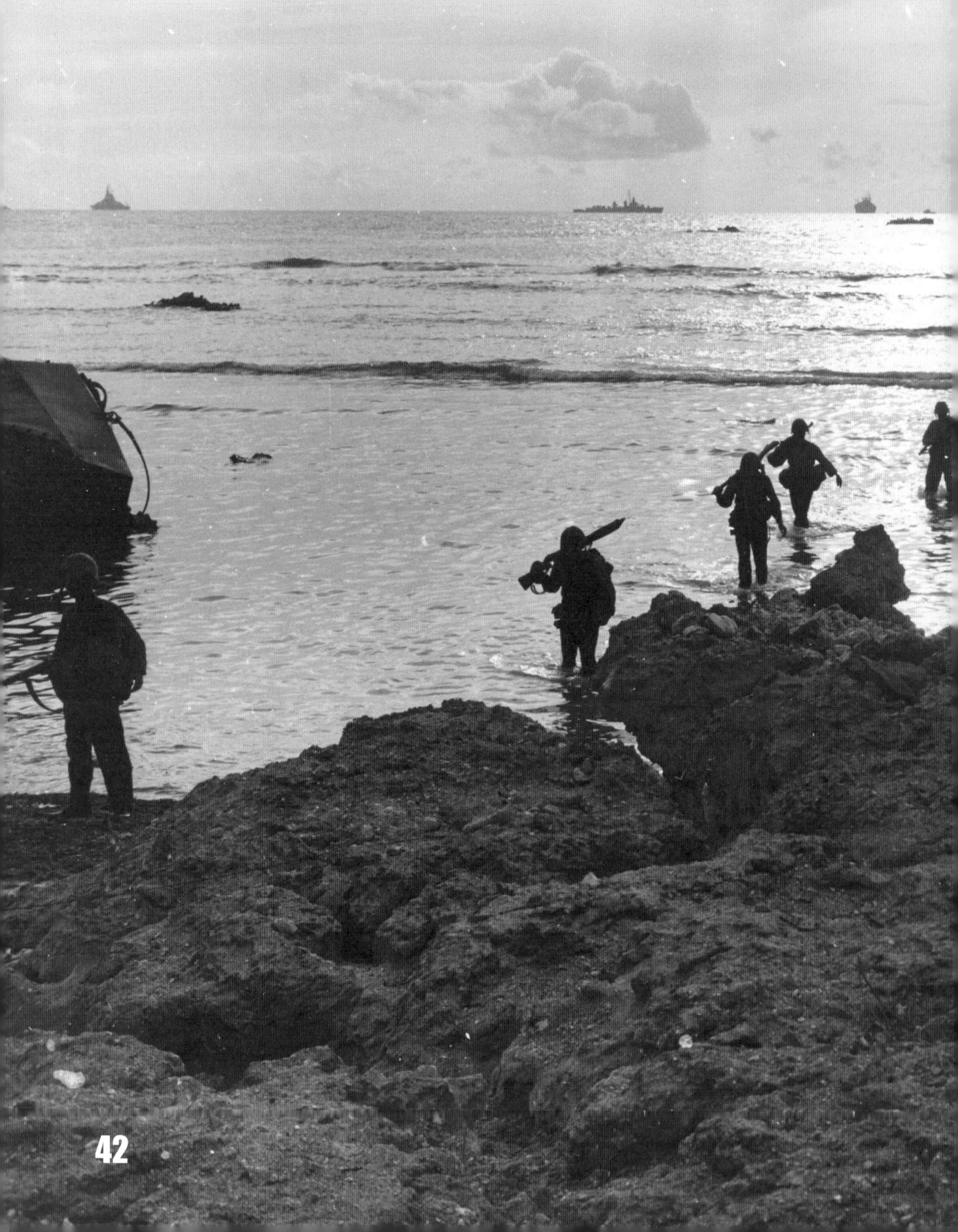

Previous page: Having been unloaded from a US Coastguard-manned landing craft, US Marines 'wade through a golden, shallow surf to hit the beach of Tinian Island … In this striking sunrise silhouette, units of a mighty task force stand on the horizon. In closer, smaller invasion craft are halted by shallow water about 100 yards off shore.' The latter description suggests that this picture might well have been taken at White 2 beach. (USNHHC)

Above: The invasion of Tinian underway as US Marines dismount from an LVT after it had been halted by the coral reef, presumably at White 2 beach, on 24 July 1944. (USNHHC)

Right: An aerial view of LVTs unloading Marines on either White 1 or White 2 on 24 July 1944. The original caption notes that 'Marines can be seen strung out in foxholes only a few yards from the beach'. (USMC Archives)

Main image: Many of the US Marines who went ashore on Tinian on 24 July 1944 did so 'feet dry'. Those seen here, however, were forced to do so 'feet wet', wading up the shallow seabed towards dry land with their weapons raised above their heads. (NARA)

Above: The same group of US Marines seen in the last picture having been photographed moments later – and a few strides closer to their landing beach on Tinian. (NARA)

Above: USS *Colorado* pictured off Tinian, having suffered damage from Japanese guns ashore, on 24 July 1944. Although the Japanese 6-inch guns were unable to penetrate *Colorado*'s armoured vitals, the effects topside among the anti-aircraft guns were severe, with seven of the guns being knocked out. For maintaining his ship off the landing beaches, and 'displaying personal courage, leadership and determination', the captain of *Colorado* was awarded the Navy Cross. Two other members of the crew were similarly decorated. This included Gunners' Mate 2/C Albert Stredney, who 'fearlessly and unhesitatingly assisting in tearing open blazing ammunition ready boxes fired by enemy shelling, Stredney aided in extinguishing the flames, thereby preventing a serious explosion which undoubtedly would have killed many men and damaged his ship'. (US Navy)

Below: As *Colorado* continued to be hit, the destroyer USS *Norman Scott*, some 1,800 yards offshore, manoeuvred to draw fire away from the battleship. In so doing, the destroyer was hit by Japanese 6-inch shells six times in just fifteen minutes. One shell was a direct hit on the bridge, which killed the commanding officer (Commander Seymore D. Owens), the officer of the deck, and the rest of the bridge team. Altogether, the shells killed twenty-two men and wounded fifty more, including seriously wounding the executive officer. USS *Norman Scott* is pictured here in October 1944, following a period of repair and refit after the Tinian operation. (USNHHC)

Above: US Navy Seabees man a pontoon barge that is being used as a mobile floating refuelling point for amphibious tractors and DUKWs off Tinian during the initial assault on the island. (National Museum of the US Navy)

Right: An M4 Sherman medium tank of the 2nd Tank Battalion, nicknamed *Corsair*, moves off the beachhead on Tinian while still fitted with deep fording trunks, 24 July 1944.

Below: Despite the damage it sustained, USS *Colorado* identified the offending Japanese battery and returned fired on it. In this it was supported by the light cruiser USS *Cleveland*, with her rapid-fire 6-inch guns, and the destroyer USS *Remey*. This effort silenced the Japanese gunners for the time being. However, the battery was not completely put out of action until 28 July, when the Pearl Harbor survivor USS *Tennessee* fired on it with a devastating combination of seventy 14-inch and 150 5-inch shells. The USS *Cleveland* is pictured here underway prior to the invasion of Tinian (USNHHC)

Below: A steady stream of LVTs and DUKWs continued to ferry ashore men, equipment and supplies throughout the first day of the American invasion of Tinian, 24 July 1944. In this aerial photograph, the vessels are seen both heading towards the beach, as well as returning back out to the ships offshore to reload. Note the Japanese airfield in the distance. (USMC Archives)

Left: Some of the DUKWs and LVTs pictured on one of the Tinian landing beaches on Jig-Day. 'Despite drizzling rain, narrow beaches, and undiscovered mines,' notes the historian Richard Harwood, that day '15,600 troops were put ashore along with great quantities of material and equipment that included four battalions of artillery, two dozen half-tracks mounting 75mm guns, and 48 medium and 15 flame-throwing tanks'. (NARA)

Main image: An orderly column of LVTs ferrying men and equipment ashore during the landings on Tinian. (NARA)

Main image: Stores and supplies are brought ashore on Tinian on Jig-Day. This image shows US Marines unloading oil drums that had been transported to the beach by US Coastguard-manned LVTs. 'Offshore,' notes the original caption, 'stands a concentration of the American invasion armada including lighters, alligators, LSTs and LCVPs'. All supplies had received special attention to prevent any congestion on the beaches. According to logistics plans, all supplies were brought across the beaches in tractors and DUKWs and taken directly to division dumps without rehandling. (NARA)

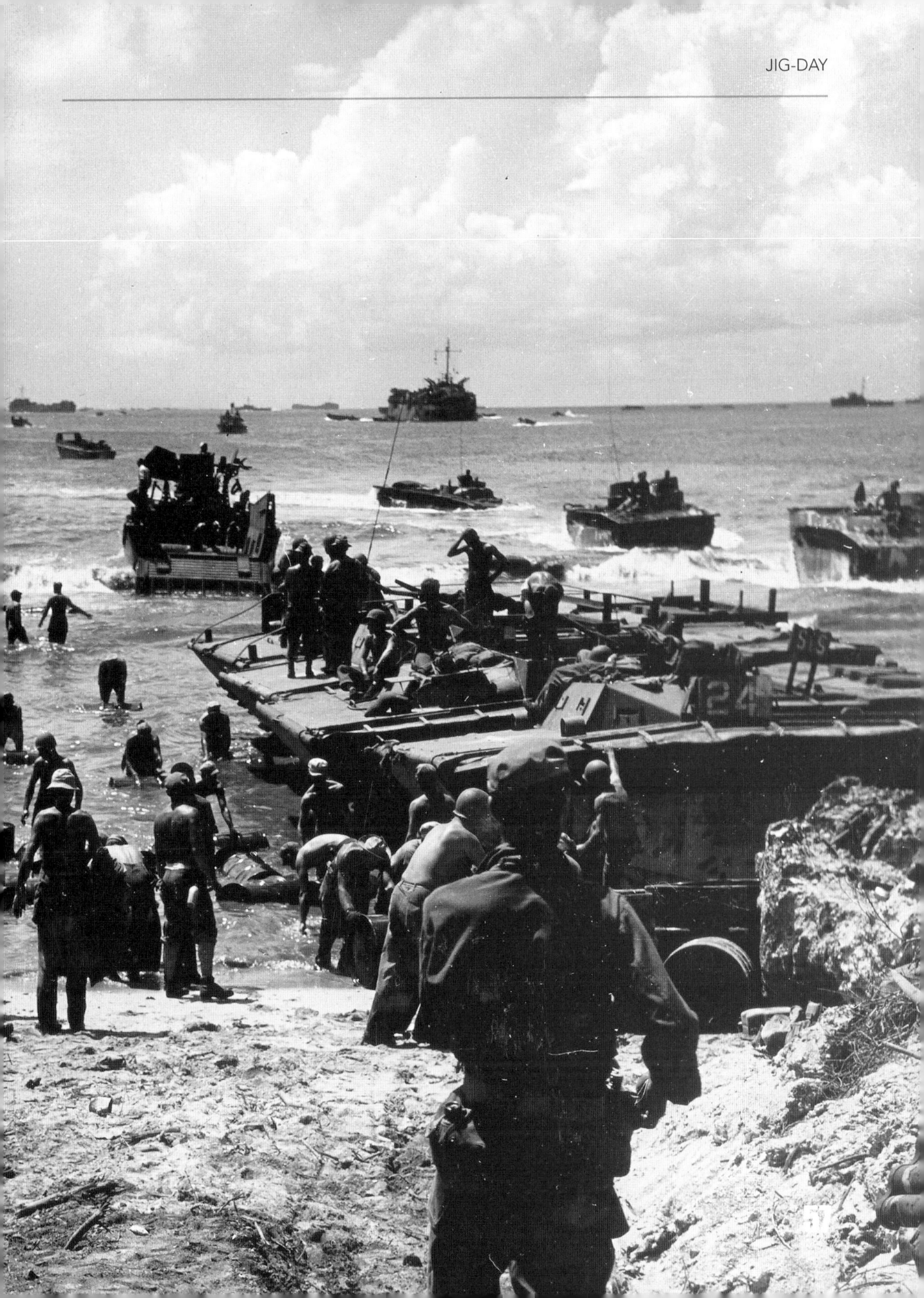
24

Above: USS LST-340 at the pontoon pier on White 2 Beach during the landings on Tinian. 'On 29 July,' notes one account, 'LST 340 was unloading trucks and embarking wounded at White Beach #2. Heavy rains and high winds whipped the water, and the sea rolled in extremely heavy swells. When the ship attempted to retract from the beach, she was caught by the wind and swells and broached, suffering heavy damage.' (National Museum of the US Navy)

Chapter 4

THE INEVITABLE COUNTER-ATTACK

25 July 1944

The attack which the Japanese hoped would drive the Americans back to their ships was the responsibility of Ogata's mobile reserve battalion (the 1st Battalion, 135th Infantry Regiment), the 1st Battalion, 50th Infantry, and sundry naval units stationed in the northern part of the island. Small numbers of these personnel had been spotted along the Marines' front during the early part of the night trying, no doubt, to assess the position and strength of the American defence.

Having learnt from bitter experience, the Marines, though, were well prepared for the impending onslaught. As well as the previously mentioned precautions, pre-loaded amphibian tractors continued to rumble ashore delivering ammunition to the men holding the beachhead, and mortars were hastily sighted to cover 'dead spots' in the defensive perimeter.

Clear indications of what was about to happen were soon apparent, as Lieutenant Colonel Justice M. Chambers, commander of the 3rd Battalion, 25th Marines, recalled: 'There was a big gully that ran from the southeast to northwest and right into the western edge of our area. Anybody in their right mind could have figured that if there was to be any counterattacks, that gully would be used

Below: A grisly scene that shows the bodies of fallen Japanese soldiers on one of Tinian's battlefields – possibly after the counter-attacks on 25 July 1944. (USMC Archives)

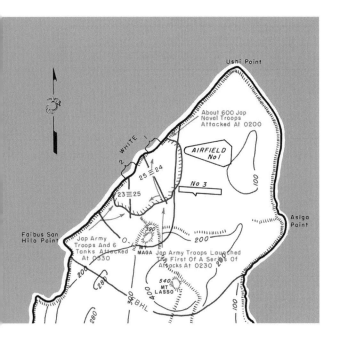

Top left: A map showing the situation on the beachhead at midnight on Jig-Day, as well as the approximate points where the Japanese counter-attacks struck.

Bottom left: For his actions during the early hours of 25 July 1944, Corporal Alfred J. Daigle was posthumously awarded the Navy Cross.

His citation states the following:

'A vigilant leader, Corporal Daigle immediately took control of the machine gun when his gunner was wounded during the fierce countermeasures initiated by the Japanese following our assault and subsequent establishment of a beachhead on this strategic island.

'Pouring a steady hail of bullets on the hostile troops, he succeeded in inflicting heavy casualties and in forcing the enemy's temporary withdrawal. Then, holding stoutly against the second attempt to penetrate our lines despite the loss of all rifle protection around his installation by concentrated hostile mortar, Machine gun and grenade fire, he continued to man his gun with cool courage, maintaining a ceaseless barrage of devastating fire against the oncoming Japanese.

'Determined not to yield his position when the emplacement was finally knocked out by hostile guns, he remained steadfast, fearlessly engaging the enemy in hand-to-hand combat and battling with fierce aggressiveness until, overpowered by the fanatic opposition, he fell, mortally injured, with one hundred of the enemy lying dead before his gun position and an additional six within the emplacement.

'An indomitable fighter, Corporal Daigle, by his intrepid initiative and resolute fortitude in the face of almost certain death, contributed essentially to the virtual annihilation of a Japanese infantry company and to the rapid consolidation of the beachhead.' (USNHHC)

… During the night … my men were reporting that they were hearing a lot of Japanese chattering down in the gully.'

At around midnight, the intermittent fire of mortar rounds upon the American positions was added to by shelling from Japanese field guns. 'They hit us about midnight in K Company's area,' continued Chambers. 'They hauled by hand a couple of 75mm howitzers with them and when they got them up to where they could fire at us, they hit us very hard.' The tempo of the Japanese shelling gradually increased until 02.00 hours. It was then that the predicted attack materialised.

It was on the left of the Marine line, where the 24th Marines were posted, that the Japanese were first spotted approaching, a small group being detected in the dark. In moments, that small group became 'a screaming mass of attackers' as some 600 Japanese naval personnel rushed forward.

The Marines shot flares into the sky, illuminating both the battlefield and the saki-crazed attackers. The defenders could hardly miss, but the Japanese would not give up and the commander of 24th's

Overleaf: A 75mm howitzer, manned by men of the 4th Marine Division, near a beach on Tinian. (US Signal Corps Archive)

Below: A wounded Marine is placed aboard an LVT for evacuation from Tinian. Note the Corpsman holding a plasma bottle. (USNHHC)

Above: An aerial of the landing flotilla taken on 25 July 1944. (NARA)

Right: For his actions in the face of the Japanese counter-attacks, Private First Class Orville H. Showers was posthumously awarded the Silver Star.

The citation contains the following detail:
   'Braving a terrific concentration of machine-gun and sniper fire when the entire crew of one machine gun became casualties, Private First Class Showers fearlessly left his protected position and, put it in operation and maintained a steady stream of fire in a valiant effort to clean out a force of Japanese troops who had infiltrated our lines.
   'Although seriously wounded during the furious action, he continued to pour his devastating barrages on the enemy and succeeded in inflicting heavy casualties before he himself was fatally struck down by a burst from a Japanese weapon.' (USNHHC)

1st Battalion, which bore the brunt of this attack, was forced to call on naval shore party personnel, engineers and literally anyone who could fire a rifle to keep the enemy at bay.

Because their communications had been wrecked by the pre-invasion bombardment, the Japanese attack was delivered in three uncoordinated thrusts. The one in the centre, which was supported by a pair of 75mm guns that the Japanese man-handled forward, was directed near the boundary between the 24th and 25th Marines. Despite sustaining heavy casualties, the impetus of the Japanese charge carried them through a weak point between the two regiments, and about 200 of them penetrated deep into the beachhead.

Below: A Japanese Type 95 Ha-Go tank, of the 9th Tank Regiment, pictured after being knocked out during the fighting on Tinian. The tanks knocked out during the counter-attacks on 25 July represented roughly half of those available to Ogata and his men.

Lieutenant Jim Lucas, a professional reporter who enlisted in the Marine Corps, recalled the Japanese tanks' advance: 'The three lead tanks broke through our wall of fire. One began to glow blood-red, turned crazily on its tracks and careened into a ditch. A second, mortally wounded, turned its machine guns on its tormentors, firing into the ditches in a last desperate effort to fight its way free. One hundred yards more and it stopped dead in its tracks. The third tried frantically to turn and then retreat, but our men closed in, literally blasting it apart … Bazookas knocked out a fourth tank with a direct hit which killed the driver. The rest of the crew piled out of the turret screaming. The fifth tank, completely surrounded, attempted to flee. Bazookas made short work of it. Another hit set it afire and its crew was cremated.' (NARA)

'When the Japs hit the rear areas, all the artillery and machine guns started shooting like hell,' continued Chambers. 'Their fire was coming from the rear and grazing right up over our heads ... In the meantime, the enemy ... was putting up a hell of a fight within 75 yards of where I was and there wasn't a damn thing I could do about it.'[16]

Eventually, these Japanese were wiped out by Marine artillerymen and elements of the 2nd Marine Division that had only just started to land on the beach.

Two of Chambers' men – Corporal Alfred J. Daigle and Private First Class Orville H. Showers – were manning a machine-gun position in the battalion's front line. A combat correspondent with the Marines described their actions: '[The two men] held their fire until the Japanese were 100 yards away, then opened up. The Japanese charged, screaming, "Banzai," firing light machine guns and throwing hand grenades. It seemed impossible that the two Marines – far ahead of their own lines – could hold on ... The next morning they were found slumped over their weapons, dead. No less than 251 Japanese bodies were piled in front of them.'[17]

The last Japanese push of their counter-attack was made at around 03.30 hours against the right of the Marines' line. It was led by five or six of the enemy's light tanks which clattered up from the direction of Tinian Town with infantry riding on them, the rest following behind on foot.

The Marines' artillery opened fire on the tanks and, as pre-arranged, US warships fired star-shells into the sky, illuminating the whole area. 'The three lead tanks broke through our wall of fire,' recalled Lieutenant Jim G. Lucas. 'One began to glow blood-red, turned crazily on its tracks, and careened into a ditch. A second, mortally wounded, turned its machine guns on its tormentors, firing into the ditches in a last desperate effort to fight its way free. One hundred yards more and it stopped dead in its tracks.

The third tried, frantically, to turn and then retreat, but our men closed in, literally blasting it apart ... Bazookas knocked out the fourth tank with a direct hit which killed the driver. The rest of the crew piled out of the turret, screaming. The fifth tank, completely surrounded, attempted to flee. Bazookas made short work of it. Another hit set it afire, and its crew was cremated.'[18]

The fighting was brutal, but the Japanese were outnumbered and outgunned. As their tactics were predictable and entirely unsophisticated, there could only be one outcome.

As had so often been the case elsewhere during the fighting in the Pacific, those Japanese who had survived were not allowed to accept defeat and conduct a tactical withdrawal. They had to succeed or die, which led to a bizarre end to the battle. This was described by Major J.W. Sperry: 'As it began to get light, Jap bodies began to fly ten to fifteen feet in the air in the area in front of our lines ... We knew that hand grenades did not have the power to blow a man's body that high and could not figure out what was happening.

'[Later] we moved out to mop up ... It turned out that about fifty percent of the dead Japs carried magnetic mines and had obviously been ordered to break through our lines and destroy the tanks in the rear of us ... The Japs who were wounded and unable to flee were placing the tank mines under their bodies and tapping the detonators.'[19]

On the morning of the 25th, the bodies of some 267 Japanese dead were counted, littering the ground in this sector. Overall, 1,241 Japanese bodies lay strewn across the battlefield, around 700 of whom were from Ogata's infantry battalions. In the fruitless counter-attack Ogata had sacrificed around one-seventh of all the men available to him, a total which represented one-fifth of his trained infantry. He had also lost almost roughly half – five – of his tanks.

Right: A pair of curious Marines pause to inspect a wrecked Japanese Type 95 Ha-Go tank. (NARA)

Above: Heavy clouds of black smoke rise from Tinian as Republic P-47s of the 318th Fighter Group 'dropped the new "gel gas" bombs on the island', 25 July 1944. (NARA)

Chapter 5

SECURING THE NORTH

25–26 July 1944

As Major General Clifton B. Cates viewed the ghastly scene that presented itself as dawn broke on the morning of 25 July, the 4th Division commander remarked that his men, through their stout defence of the previous few hours, 'broke the Japs back in the battle for Tinian'. It was unquestionably the case that Ogata had sacrificed most of his mobile reserve without purpose and the capture of the island, though not a formality, was now pretty much a certainty.

Below: Taken by Technical Sergeant H. Neil Gillespie, this image shows US Marines advancing through a village on Tinian during the search for Japanese snipers. The buildings were, notes the original caption, fired by artillery. (NARA)

Left: A US Marines' machine-gun team sets up in the cover of a cliff on Tinian. (US Signal Corps Archive)

The Marines' next move was to seal off the northern part of the island so that they could concentrate on bringing the airfield at Ushi Point under their control. This would help facilitate resupply and evacuation operations, as well as neutralize the enemy's strongpoints on Mount Maga and Mount Lasso. Once this had been achieved, the Marines could then push south to take the rest of the island.

During the day, the remainder of the 4th Marine Division came ashore followed by the rest of the 2nd Marine Division as well as more of the tanks of the 2nd Tank Battalion, including a number of deadly flame-throwers. Only the occasional shell from Japanese 75mm guns disturbed the otherwise perfunctory landings of men, machines, and matériel. At the same time, the 23rd Regiment moved off northwards along the coast, mopping up isolated pockets of Japanese infantry as it went.

The 8th Regiment advanced towards Ushi Point, eliminating survivors of the night battle as they went. By the afternoon the former enemy airfield was in its possession.

At the same time, the 25th Regiment pushed inland towards Mount Maga. The northern face of this height formed an almost sheer 390-foot cliff, but the east and west approaches were far less formidable. The 25th's Commanding Officer, Colonel Merton J. Batchelder, therefore, undertook a typical pincer movement, placing his 2nd Battalion in front of the northern cliff to hold the attention of the enemy, while his other two battalions swept round from the left and the right to take the position from the flanks.

As the 1st and 2nd battalions moved up the side of the hill they came under small arms fire. Rather than risk unnecessary casualties, Batchelder asked the attached platoon of medium and light tanks to take out the hill's

Above: Bombs explode on Tinian Island on 25 July 1944. The photograph was taken by the crew of an aircraft operation from USS *White Plains* (CVE 66). (National Museum of the US Navy)

Below: A portrait of Colonel Merton Jennings Batchelder, USMC. A veteran of the fighting on Kwajalein and Saipan, for his 'extraordinary heroism as Commanding Officer of the 25th Marines, 4th Marine Division, during action against enemy Japanese forces at Tinian', Batchelder was subsequently awarded the Navy Cross. His citation includes the following description of his actions during the Tinian operations: 'Landing on the heavily fortified beachhead with the first assault wave on D-Day in the face of intense, concentrated enemy mortar, machine-gun and artillery fire, Colonel Batchelder

fearlessly directed his command in seizing the vital area, establishing a beachhead line and holding it against repeated vicious counterattacks by a fanatic enemy until the full force of our supporting elements could be landed. Continuing his unceasing efforts, he contributed to the success of his regiment in repelling a determined pre-dawn counterattack the following day and, thereafter, supervised brilliantly executed, daily attacks against a ruthless and determined enemy, remaining in the field with his front line troops through the entire operation, inspiring his men to greater efforts and coordinating the activities of his regiment in capturing this vital Japanese stronghold. His valiant leadership, outstanding fortitude and great personal valor, maintained at great personal risk, reflect the highest credit upon Colonel Batchelder.' (via Historic Military Press)

defenders. The only way the tanks could mount the hill was along a single road, which the Japanese had mined. Engineers from the 20th Marines immediately began a clearance operation and soon reported the road ready for use.

The tanks set off, reached the top of the hill, only to return without finding any of the enemy. But when the Marines began to climb the slopes once more, they again came under fire. This time, though, the exact position of the enemy was observed and, from the base of the hill, the guns of the M4 Shermans blasted the top of the hill. Mount Maga was then taken without further opposition.

However, the 25th came under mortar, rifle, and machine-gun fire from a plateau 200 yards to the south. This position was strafed and bombed by a squadron of USAAF P-47s and, as the 23rd Regiment came into line with the 25th, the opposition they encountered was neutralized by gunfire from the battleship USS *California*.

The P-47s were carrying napalm, the use of which Major General Cates witnessed for the first time: 'The first morning they put it down, I went up to the front line and those planes came in over our heads it seemed to me like about a hundred feet in the air … [They] let go their napalm bombs right over our heads … maybe two or three hundred yards in front of us. It was a very devastating thing and particularly to the morale of the Japanese.' Each bomb cleared an area approximately seventy-five by 200 feet and, in some cases, left behind little but the charred bodies of Japanese troops.[20]

With Mount Maga secured, the route to the other major objective, Mount Lasso, had been cleared. Taking that height, though, would have to wait until the next day. The Marines duly dug in for the night, wary that the Japanese might make another of their infamous counter-attacks.

Otaga had learnt his lesson, it would seem, as there was no repeat of the previous night, though the Americans were harassed continually by small numbers of Japanese trying to infiltrate their lines. The only result of those efforts was more dead Japanese. The only confrontation of note saw a slightly larger group of Japanese approach the positions held by the 24th Marines. They were spotted by the reconnaissance platoon.

'We opened up and let them have it as fast as we could pull our triggers,' recalled Lieutenant Victor Maghakian. 'They began screaming … and making awful noises. Then after a few minutes I ordered my platoon to fall back to the division lines because I was afraid that maybe our own division might fire on us. After falling back, I reported what happened, and our troops opened up … with mortar and machine gun fire.' Between thirty-five and forty dead Japanese were counted the next morning.

The key operation of Day 3 of the invasion was the securing of Mount Lasso. From this 540-foot peak the Japanese were able to observe the beachhead and direct artillery and mortar fire on the American rear areas. The task of taking Mount Lasso was handed to the 4th Division, while the 2nd Division was ordered to consolidate the areas around Ushi Point airfield.

The attack on Mount Lasso began at 07.55 hours on 26 July with a bombardment from all thirteen battalions of XXIV Corps' artillery, plus the guns of the battleship USS *Tennessee* and the light cruiser USS *Cleveland*. Just five minutes later the Marines moved forward.

Meeting very little opposition, the 23rd and 25th regiments advanced quickly through the fields of sugar cane. Reaching the bottom of the mountain, the 1st Battalion of the 25th scrambled up the steep and rugged slopes. They reached the top to find the mountain deserted. Ogata had abandoned the island's highest point without a fight.

As for the 2nd Division, after the 8th Regiment had flushed out any enemy stragglers around the airfield, it was joined by the 2nd Regiment and together they pushed across the island to reach Tinian's east coast. The north of the island had been secured ahead of schedule and the drive south could begin. The operation on Tinian was going better than planned.

Main image: US troops pushing out over some of Tinian's flat, more open countryside, ever mindful of Japanese snipers and stragglers. (NARA)

Above: The Assistant Division Commander of the 2nd Marine Division, Brigadier General Merritt A. Edson, holding the binoculars, follows the progress of his troops 'not far from the scene of the action'. Having attained the rank of Brigadier General in December 1943, Edson was awarded the Silver Star for service in Saipan and Tinian, having been awarded the Medal of Honor for his actions during the fighting on Guadalcanal. (NARA)

Opposite page top: Marines securing one of the airfields on Tinian. This is possibly that at Ushi Point. (NARA)

Opposite page bottom: Marines move across the wrecked landscape that is Ushi Point airfield on the northern end of Tinian Island as they continue their mopping up operations. (USMC Archives)

Above: US troops cover the entrance to a Japanese bunker, almost certainly a posed image that was taken at Ushi Point airfield. Note the distinctive air raid shelters in the background, structures which can still be seen today. (USMC Archives)

Below: The shell of a hangar at Ushi Point airfield pictured soon after its capture. (USMC Archives)

Chapter 6

THE DRIVE SOUTH

26–30 July 1944

Persistent activity by the Japanese throughout the night of 26/27 July meant that there was no relaxation in the vigilance of the Marines. However, there were no major attempts at penetrating the perimeter. The exception involved a small group of enemy personnel which had become trapped behind the American lines and which used the cover of night to break out to join their comrades. Small and local though the night's actions had been, dawn still broke to reveal 137 Japanese dead sprawled ahead and behind the Marine's perimeter.

With the north reasonably secure, the Marines' advance south began at 07.30 hours on 27 July. It was the 2nd Division which took the lead after another five-minute barrage on locations likely to harbour the enemy. Preceded by tanks to eliminate any unsubdued Japanese strongpoints, the Marines encountered very little opposition and the day's objective was

Below: Supported by an M-4 Sherman, US Marines continue their advance on Tinian. (NARA)

achieved by early afternoon. The men settled down to what was a relatively untroubled night's rest.

The next day it was the turn of the 4th Division to form the vanguard of the continued push south. Once again, it moved out after a brief artillery barrage, also with tanks to the fore. As on the 27th, there was almost no opposition to the American advance, Otaga's men having withdrawn to the hills and caves on the southern coast. The Americans had no means of knowing this and had to advance with caution, particularly with regards to Otaga's main infantry body, the 50th Regiment.

'It is believed that this unit is largely intact, and it is known that they are well-equipped and seasoned troops,' calculated the V Amphibious Corps' Intelligence Officer, Thomas R. Yancey. 'They are capable of intervention at any time and may be expected to offer a strong opposition when encountered.'[21] But the American advance caught almost 200 Japanese civilians who had not withdrawn in time, and under interrogation they revealed that Otaga had pulled back to the south. With this in mind, Major General Schmidt abandoned his cautious approach and, on the 29th, both divisions were ordered to advance as quickly as they could, the 2nd Division on the left of the line and the 4th on the right.

Behind the front line in the days since the initial landings, more troops and artillery had reached Tinian, and with a round-the-clock effort from logistical personnel who moved huge quantities of water, ammunition and rations across the narrow beaches, the momentum of the Marines' advance was maintained unrestrained by supply limitations. Ushi Point airfield, which had intentionally been spared from the preliminary bombardment on Jig-Day, was already in use by artillery observation aircraft, and the 121st Naval Construction Battalion was hard at work improving and extending its runway.

It rained heavily throughout the night of 29/30 July and the Japanese sought to take advantage of the downpour to close in on the Marines' positions. But the rain had kept the men awake and they heard the enemy gathering for what was presumed to be an attack. When mortar rounds began to fall in their midst, they were ready to reply in kind, with artillery also being called upon to scour the ground beyond the perimeter. The attack was thwarted and next morning the sun shone on forty-one dead Japanese.

As the Marines advanced that day, Jig+6, the 1st Battalion, 24th Regiment, on the right of the 4th Division, came up against several Japanese machine-gunners and riflemen holed up in caves near the coast. These were eliminated ruthlessly, with M4 Shermans from Company B, 4th Tank Battalion blasting the enemy's position while light flame-thrower tanks moved in closer to pour their deadly fire, quite literally, through the entrances of the caves. Then, covered by USMC riflemen and machine-gunners, combat engineers moved up to the caves with flame-throwers, explosive charges and bazookas to finish off any survivors.

During this fighting there was one remarkable act of courage. Private Joseph W. Ozbourn, a rifleman equipped with a Browning Automatic Rifle serving in the 1st Battalion, 23rd Regiment, was one of those assigned the task of clearing the Japanese out of the caves. 'As a member of a platoon assigned the mission of clearing the remaining Japanese troops from dugouts and pillboxes along a tree line,' notes one official account, 'Private Ozbourn, flanked by two men on either side, was moving forward to throw an armed hand grenade into a dugout when a terrific blast from the entrance severely wounded the four men and himself. Unable to throw the grenade into the dugout and with no place to hurl it without endangering the other men, Private Ozbourn unhesitatingly

Right: A Republic P-47 Thunderbolt of the 19th Fighter Squadron, 318th Fighter Group, taking-off from Saipan for a strafing mission over Tinian, 26 July 1944. (NARA)

grasped it close to his body and fell upon it, sacrificing his own life to absorb the full impact of the explosion but saving his comrades.' For his actions Ozbourn was posthumously awarded the Medal of Honor.

With these positions neutralized the 4th Division entered Tinian Town early in the afternoon of 30 July. The place had been all but demolished by the preliminary naval and air bombardment and only one Japanese soldier was found alive in its ruins, though he was killed the moment he was discovered.

The 2nd Division had a more difficult day, coming under fire from machine-guns and a 70mm howitzer as it moved down the eastern side of the island. The 2nd Division's 3rd Battalion was soon engaged in 'its busiest period of the entire Tinian operation'. The unit's Commanding Officer, Lieutenant Colonel Walter F. Layer, later gave the following account: 'On or about 1230, 30 July 1944, [we] were temporarily halted by machine gun and 70mm gun fire coming from the right front of the battalion's zone of action. Captain Robert F. O'Brien, commanding officer of Love Company ... dispatched a patrol which destroyed the enemy guns and crews ...

'After Captain O'Brien's patrol had destroyed the guns that held up the battalion, the attack was continued across an open field approximately two hundred yards wide where on the far side approximately ten well constructed machine gun positions were captured complete with the guns. The enemy had abandoned these positions and had retreated approximately one hundred yards south. They moved down a steep cliff, approximately eighty feet high, via a dirt road into a large cave running back north under the cliff.

'Marines of Love Company pursued the enemy, chasing them into the afore-mentioned

Right: Marines, one armed with a pistol, gingerly approach a Japanese position during mopping up actions on Tinian. (US Signal Corps Archive)

cave. The enemy were contained in the cave until the entire 3d Battalion advanced down the cliff and had taken positions ready to continue the attack. [I] requested and received from the commanding officer, 2d Marines the assistance of a flame-throwing tank which along with Marines from the 3d Battalion destroyed approximately eighty enemy and approximately four machine guns [in] the afore-mentioned cave. As the cave was being attacked, enemy forces approximately five hundred yards to our front (south) deployed in rocky terrain took the 3d Battalion, 2d Marines, under fire with mortars.

'It is beyond my memory as to the number of casualties the 3d Battalion suffered at that time. I personally rendered first aid to two wounded Marines and remember seeing six or seven Marines who were either wounded or killed by that enemy mortar fire. Tanks and half-tracks that were attached to the 3d Battalion, 2d Marines, took the enemy under fire, destroying the enemy mortars.'[22]

Further enemy resistance was met when the division reached the 340-foot hill on Masalog Point. There, one group of Japanese was ensconced in caves on the high ground. The hill was assaulted and by 17.15 hours the western portion of the heights was in American hands. At this point Major General Watson decided to dig in for the night.

By this point in the campaign, the Marines 'had advanced so rapidly that only four square miles of the island remained for safe firing by ships not supporting battalions [i.e., not with shore spotters],' noted Rear Admiral Harry W. Hill in a report on 30 July.

Roughly four-fifths of the island of Tinian were now in American hands. It had taken the Marines less than a week.

Right: US Marines stack mortar rounds in preparation for firing a fast barrage on Tinian during the fighting on 30 July 1944. (USNHHC)

Main image: The truck-mounted 4.5-inch rocket launchers of the 1st and 2nd Provisional Rocket companies in action on Tinian. Note one of the rockets can just be seen in the air above the half-track on the left. One account states that, 'Although frontline Marines appreciated the support [of the] rocket launchers, they always dreaded the period immediately following a barrage. The dust and smoke thrown up at that time served as a perfect aiming point for enemy artillery and mortars which soon followed.' (NARA)

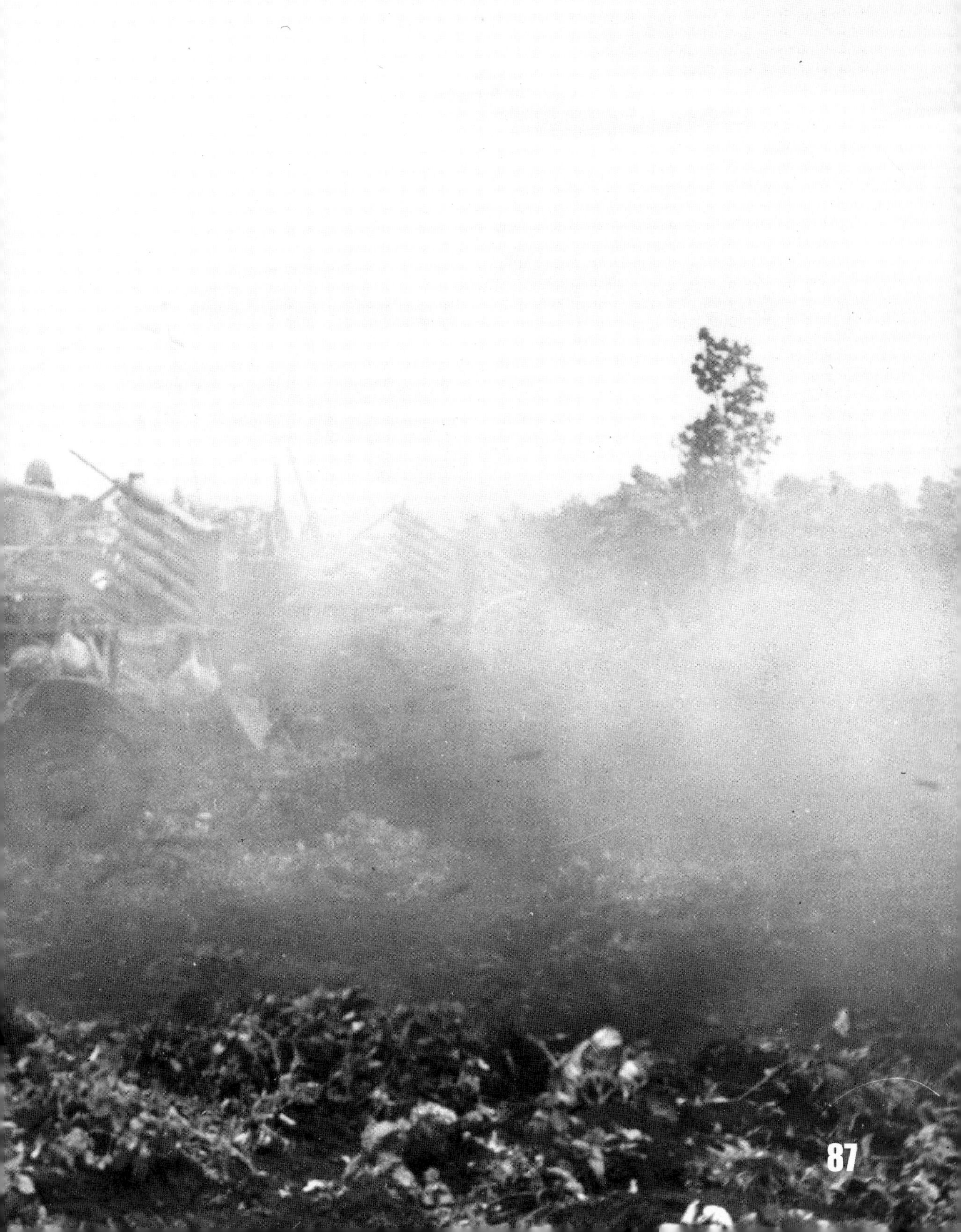

Left: Medal of Honor recipient Private Joseph William Ozbourn. Ozbourn was initially buried on Tinian, though his remains were subsequently re-interred in the National Cemetery of the Pacific in Honolulu.

Right: In the words of the original wartime caption, this image shows the 'Battle of the Cane Fields' underway on Tinian. Pushing across the island, 'the US Marines wage a fight from cane field to cane field against Japanese snipers. The smoke is from cane fields set afire to drive the enemy into the open.' (NARA)

Below: Marines advance through a cane field on Tinian as they 'push the Japanese deeper and deeper into the southern tip of the island'. (NARA)

Above: A column of US Marines advancing down one of Tinian's main roads. (USMC Archives)

Chapter 7

'A VIOLENT, FRONTAL SURGE'

31 July 1944

From the interrogation of a captured Japanese NCO, it was estimated that Otaga had already lost around 3,000 men, or approximately one-third of the Japanese forces believed to have been on Tinian. But with the Japanese concentrated, or perhaps more accurately, cornered in the south of the island, where Otaga had established his command post by a shrine in a cliff near Marpo Point, they were sure to make a defiant last stand.

As the Japanese were holed out close to the sea on such a small island, this meant that the US warships would be able to shell the enemy positions with great accuracy. So, for the attack upon the southern cliffs, a powerful flotilla was assembled just offshore.

Two destroyers were to provide direct support for each of the 2nd and 6th Regiments, seven for the 23rd, and one each for the 8th and 25th Marines. In addition, a general bombardment of the

Below: Marine Private First Class Louis P. Hart, who hailed from Philadelphia, takes cover behind a tree on Tinian. (US Signal Corps Archive)

Left: In single file Marines from the 2nd Division scale one of the cliffs or hills on Tinian, to reach the rocky plateau above, on 31 July 1944. Cutting almost the entire width of the island, this cliff was a formidable obstacle to the Marines that day. (US Signal Corps Archive)

cliffs was to be undertaken by the battleships *Tennessee* and *California*, the heavy cruiser *Louisville*, and the light cruisers *Montpelier* and *Birmingham*. General Schmidt's orders for the 31st were blunt: 'Annihilate the opposing Japanese.'

Throughout the night of 30/31 July, the artillery of the two divisions and that of XXIV Corps pounded the cliffs, a bombardment that continued as dawn broke. The warships joined in the action at 06.00 hours on the morning of 31 July, ceasing for forty minutes to allow the USAAF its turn. Every available bomb-carrying aircraft in the area, a total of 126, flew across from Aslito airfield on Saipan to drop a total of sixty-nine tons of bombs on the unfortunate enemy. As the last of the USAAF machines returned to Saipan, the warships took over again, delivering another thirty-five-minute-long bombardment. When the guns finally fell silent at 08.30 hours, more than 600 tons of shells had struck the faces of the cliffs.

The end of the barrage signalled the start of the attack by the Marines. The gentle, flat fields of the central parts of Tinian had been left behind. Now the men were facing thick scrub which hampered movement and concealed enemy snipers. So ahead of the Marines went the armour. The light flame-throwing tanks seared away both the vegetation and those concealed within it, while the guns of the medium tanks blasted enemy strongpoints and LVTs provided valuable fire support by moving along in the water abreast of the right flank of the 4th Division.

The 23rd Marines on the left of the division soon encountered small arms fire from the cliff to the left front and from a tiny village at its

Right: Marines help a Japanese soldier from a dugout on Tinian after they convinced him 'that life as a prisoner was more desirable than death for the Emperor'. He still holds the cigarette that Marines offered him while coaxing him out. (US Signal Corps Archive)

base, while in its front was fire from an unseen larger-calibre artillery piece. It was not possible for the position to be outflanked, and with the enemy gun so well concealed that its location could not be relayed to the divisional artillery, the warships offshore or the aircraft overhead, the Marines had no choice but to attack the Japanese position head-on.

The supporting tanks moved in, blasting away at likely fissures in the cliff, but without any visible result. So, by all accounts, the Marines took matters into their own hands without any instructions being issued. First one Marine would dash forward a few yards in a zig-zag run and then dive to the ground behind a rock or a bush before the enemy could train any of their weapons on the moving target. Then another would follow suit, and another. This pattern was repeated across the front until the Marines closed in upon the defenders.

Behind them Company C, 4th Tank Battalion, continued to hammer at the cliff. One tank was hit by successive rounds, as was a second. But the guns of both remained functioning and at last the position of the enemy artillery piece was spotted and quickly silenced.

During the day the division had advanced 2,500 yards. As darkness fell, the men dug in for the night at the foot of the cliff, though one company actually reached the top, spending the night there.

On the left, the 2nd Division reached the base of the cliffs with all three of its regiments in line abreast. After a day of heavy fighting and much arduous climbing, one company of the 2nd Division's 8th Regiment reached the top of the cliff by late afternoon, being joined

Main image: US personnel pick their way through the ruins of a Japanese barracks that had suffered at the hands of the American aerial and naval bombardments. (NARA)

Above: A number of those badly wounded in the fighting on Tinian were evacuated to hospital ships and the like waiting offshore. Of those who subsequently died of their injuries, many were buried at sea – such as in the ceremony pictured here. (USMC Archives)

Right: A column of US Marines advances through the devastated shell of Tinian Town, 'which bears evidence of the fury of the battle', en route to the front, 31 July 1944. (USMC Archives)

after dark by most of two other battalions of the regiment. However, as night fell, there was a gap of 600 yards on the right and one of 350 yards on the left of the Marine battalions on the top of the cliff.

'By the time we got up there,' recalled Captain Carl W. Hoffman of the 2nd Battalion, 8th Marines, 'there wasn't enough daylight left to get ourselves properly barbed-wired in, to get our fields of fire established, to site our interlocking bands of machine gun fire – all the things that should be done in preparing a good defense'.[23] Seizing the opportunity, it was a weakness Otaga set out to exploit.

As darkness continued to creep over the Pacific, the enemy started to infiltrate the Marines' lines. 'It was a completely black night,' continued Hoffman. 'So, with Japanese moving around in our positions, our troops became very edgy and were challenging everybody in sight ... As the night wore on, the intensity of enemy attacks started to build and build and build. They finally launched a full scale banzai attack against [our] battalion ...

'The strange thing the Japanese did here was that they executed one wave of attack after another against a 37mm position firing cannister ammunition ... That gun just stacked up dead Japanese ... As soon as one Marine gunner would drop another would take his place. [Eight of ten men who manned the gun were killed or wounded.] Soon we were nearly shoulder-high with dead Japanese in front of that weapon.'[24]

It has been said that Colonel Ogata personally led the attack. According to one prisoner of war, the Japanese commander was killed during the charge by American machine-guns, being last seen hanging dead over the Marines' barbed wire, though this description is not universally accepted.

About 2,300 Japanese were involved in that first attack upon the 8th Regiment. But, despite their huge losses, the Japanese were far from finished.

Some three hours after the battle a force of approximately 150 of the enemy suddenly rushed the hairpin road up which the Marines had been trying to carry ammunition and other supplies. They seized and set fire to a pair of ambulance Jeeps and blocked the road, hoping to cut off the Marines on the top of the cliff. A platoon of these Japanese even moved up the road to attack the rear of the 2nd Battalion, only being driven off after a brief but bitter hand-to-hand struggle.

This was perhaps the most dangerous moment of the invasion so far for the Americans. The battalion commander, Major William C. Chamberlin, had no idea whether this was an isolated group or the first of a large number of the enemy which might overrun the rear of the Marines while unknown numbers of Japanese were still lurking in the dark in front of him. He had to act – and quickly.

After driving off the platoon that had attacked his rear, Chamberlin mounted a counter-attack of his own, dislodging the rest of the Japanese that had blocked the road. He set up his own roadblock and for the next three hours, with the support of armour, mortars and field artillery, the battalion kept the enemy at bay.

But at 05.15 hours came the final banzai charge, again directed towards the 2nd Battalion. 'It struck against the left of Company E in a violent, frontal surge,' wrote Hoffman. 'Immediately the entire area was bathed in a bright light as mortars and ships fired illuminating shells over the area. The Marines' battle cry – "flares" – equalled in volume the screams – "banzai" – of the Japanese. As long as they could see their foes, Marines felt certain that they could stop them.

'The most effective Marine weapons during the onslaught were the two canister-coughing 37mm guns. The crews of these weapons performed magnificently; gunners became casualties and were quickly replaced; replacement gunners were hit and others took over. The turnover was tragic and monotonous. The gunshields' thin upper portions were easily pierced by point-blank small-arms fire, and no gunner remained at his post for over four or five minutes before getting hit. Still the guns were constantly and efficiently manned – never a moment's hesitation, never a lost opportunity. By daybreak only two of ten original crew members were left.'[25] The 8th Marines suffered seventy-four casualties that night, but in strewn across the front of Company E were 100 lifeless Japanese bodies.

It was clear to all, that the first day of August was likely to be the last day of the Battle of Tinian. There was nowhere for the Japanese to go, and the Americans had a firm grip on the cliff top. But exactly how the Japanese would respond remained the main concern of US commanders. Would they throw themselves at the Marines, or, as had happened so tragically at Saipan, throw themselves off the cliffs to their deaths? The next few hours and days were not going to be pleasant for either friend or foe.

Right: Marines use a flamethrower in an attempt to subdue stubborn Japanese resistance in the jungle on Tinian. (USMC Archives)

Above: Marines in what may be an improvised aid post during the fighting on Tinian. (USMC Archives)

Chapter 8

TINIAN SECURED

1–3 August 1944

Before the 2nd Marine Division launched what it expected to be its final assault on 1 August, the Japanese positions were yet again hammered from the sea and the air. For its part, the US Navy hurled a total of 615 tons of shells at the cliffs, whilst the aircraft dropped a further sixty-nine tons of explosives.

The effect of this bombardment was, according to prisoners captured in its aftermath, 'almost unbearable'. But the 2nd Division had to wait for the remaining battalions not yet up on the cliff to make the ascent and join them before they could move out. The attack was therefore delayed until 08.00 hours.

The terrain offered more resistance to the Marines than the Japanese, but by 11.50 hours the 8th Regiment was finally in position to mount the final assault on Marpo Point. It took until almost 15.00 hours for the regiment reach the edge of the cliff overlooking the sea. It seemed that every

Below: US Marines moving through one of the last villages on Tinian to be cleared of Japanese personnel, circa 1 August 1944. Evidence of the recent fighting in this area can clearly be seen. (NARA)

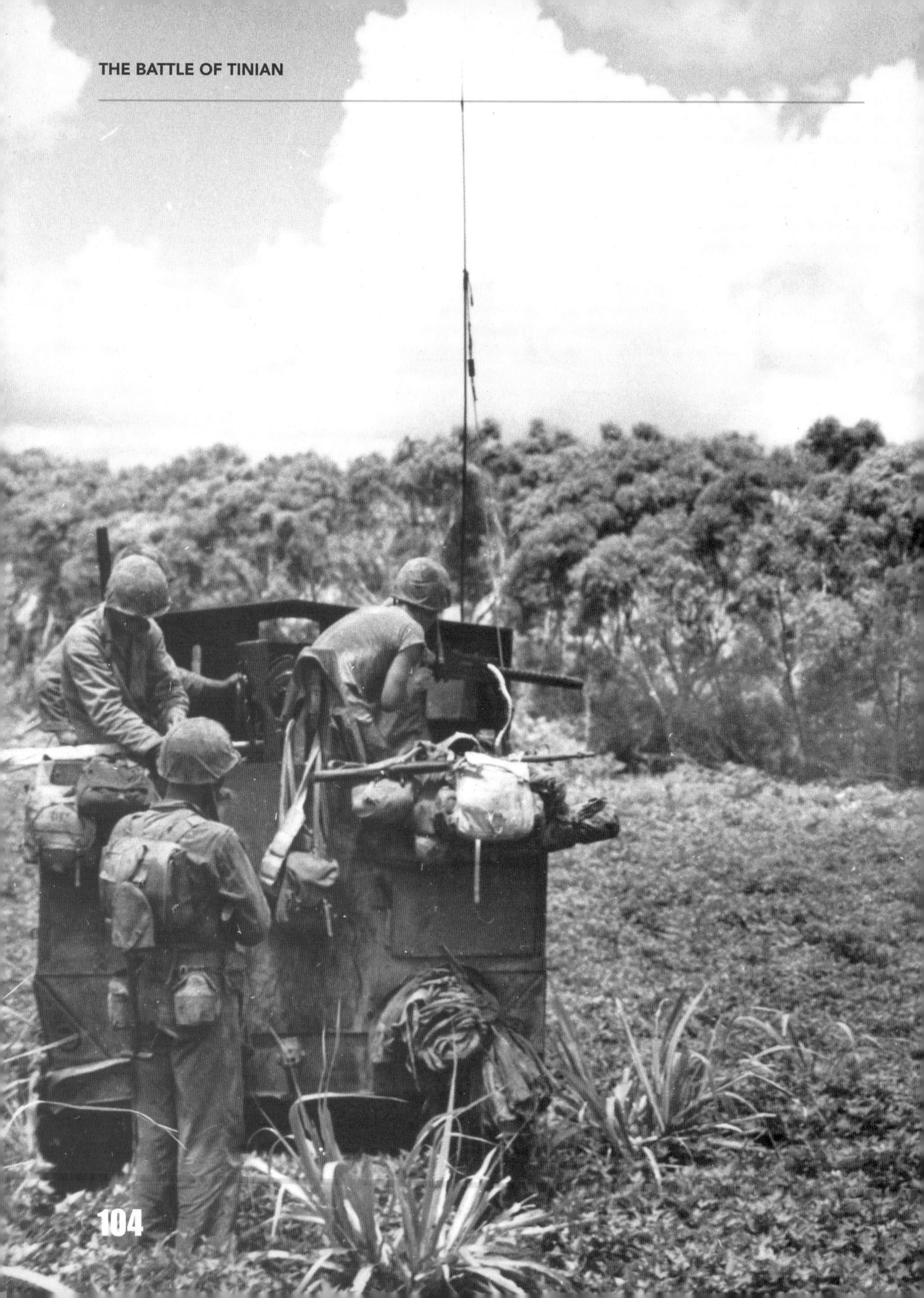

Main image: The original caption to this images states that it shows the 'small sector of the island' into which the last Japanese defenders had crowded. 'The Marines with this half-track mounting a 75mm gun,' it adds, 'are cautious as they approach the woods, in the background. They are expecting the hard pressed enemy to turn for a last desperate stand on the southern tip of the island.' (NARA)

Right: A group of Marines from a .30-calibre machine-gun squad enjoy a locally grown watermelon on Tinian, 1 August 1944. (USNHHC)

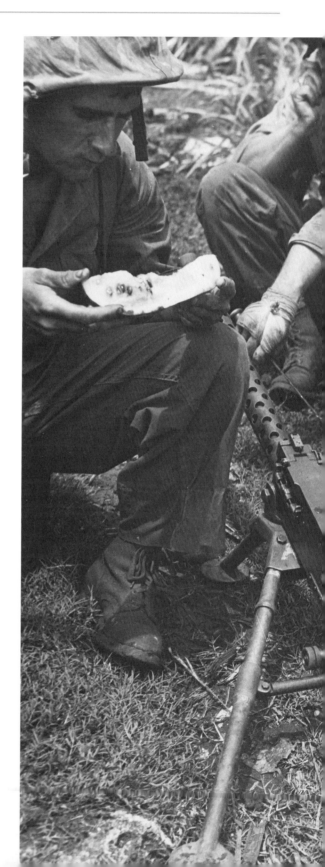

crack or fissure in the cliffs hid enemy troops who had absolutely no intention of surrendering. It was quickly becoming clear that a long mopping up operation would be needed to completely eradicate the Japanese threat on the island.

As the men of the 6th Regiment reached the coast, civilians began emerging from hideouts waving white cloths. Seeing that they were being treated humanely by the Americans, more and more civilians left their hiding places. By 15.10 hours on 1 August, the Marines were so overwhelmed with refuges that the regiment received orders to hold up for the night.

The other regiment of the 2nd Division, the 2nd, had the job of preventing any of the enemy escaping along the east coast. This was achieved without difficulty, the men digging in to consolidate their position.

The 4th Division, likewise, kicked off at 08.00 hours after another five-minute artillery bombardment. Ahead of the Marines went the tanks, crashing through the dense undergrowth and blasting away at the caves and crevices in the rocks – anywhere the enemy might lurk. The only resistance they encountered was offered by small groups of Japanese who fought stubbornly before being eliminated.

When the 24th Regiment reached the cliff edge the men saw what were described as three distinct levels, or steps, down to the sea. As they tackled each of the three steps, grenades were thrown at Marines or shots were fired from the deep caves. Despite this, the regiment's objective was reached at around 18.00 hours.

Moving parallel with its sister regiment, the 23rd encountered more serious opposition. A compact group of around fifty well-armed

Japanese opened up on the advancing Marines with machine-guns. Confident that they could match the Japanese, the Marines responded in kind with their own automatic weapons and the entire enemy group was wiped out.

The two divisions had reached the end of the island and had eliminated every organized Japanese force. Though there were unknown numbers of the enemy still hiding out in caves, General Schmidt felt able to declare the island secured at 18.55 hours on 1 August 1944.

The Americans may have considered Tinian 'secure', but that, however, was far from being the opinion of the surviving Japanese. Early on the morning of 2 August, the bedraggled but defiant remnants of Otaga's garrison set out to prove their point.

With no warning, a force of up to possibly 250 Japanese launched itself at the command post of the 3rd Battalion, 6th Marines. The first to be struck were the men in the aid station, but soon everyone in the headquarters group – clerks, signallers, corpsmen, assault engineers, mortarmen, and staff personnel – was engaged the fighting.[26] But, the pistols, carbines, and two automatic rifles available to the Marines seemed insufficient against the do-or-die attitude of the Japanese. The outcome of the fighting was uncertain until Captain John R. Steinstra, Headquarters Company commander, ran to the nearby Company F of the 2nd Battalion, 6th Marines, acquired a medium tank and a rifle platoon, and led them into the battle. Two hours of combat left 119 Japanese dead.[27]

The 2nd Battalion of the 6th Marines had its own similar battle to face that morning, though against far fewer numbers. Thirty Japanese dead were counted on its front.

Right: Men of the 302nd Construction Battalion repair a pontoon causeway that had broached at Tinian's White 2 beach during a storm, 1 August 1944. (USNHHC)

The following morning, the Japanese struck yet again. The 3rd battalions of both the 6th and 8th regiments, which were operating together, were attacked by some 150 Japanese soldiers and sailors who, wishing only 'to die in battle, rather than surrender', flung themselves at the Americans. All but a handful were killed.[28]

Further attacks followed, though with very diminished numbers on both the succeeding mornings. On 1 August it had been estimated that the mopping up on Tinian would take a week. The reality, however, was that it was a task that would take about a month to complete.

Below: Marines 'mopping up on Tinian drop into firing positions when the enemy is sighted. The Leatherneck in foreground, who took advantage of a shell crater, has just fired his rifle. The others, using a kneeling position, are ready to pull the trigger.' (NARA)

Opposite page top: Flame-throwers and demolition men move up to the cliffs and caves where the Japanese are hiding on Tinian, 2 August 1944. (US Signal Corps Archive)

Opposite page bottom: An exhausted US Marine grabs a quick 'field nap' after coming off the line on Tinian, 2 August 1944. Note the M-1 carbine laying on the ground beside him. (USNHHC)

Opposite page top: The Stars and Stripes is raised over Tinian, 3 August 1944. (USNHHC)

Opposite page bottom: A US Marine ties the halyard rope to the flagpole having just raised the US flag on Tinian on 3 August 1944. (USMC Archives)

Above: In this picture taken during the flag raising at Tinian Island on 3 August 1944, are, left to right, Brigadier General Erskine, Brigadier General Edson (back to camera), Admiral R.A. Spruance, and Rear Admiral H.W. Hill. (USNHHC)

Left: Senior US Navy and Marine Corps officers present at the flag raising ceremony on Tinian on 3 August 1944. They are, from left to right: Vice Admiral Harry W. Hill, USN; Major General Harry Schmidt, USMC; Admiral Raymond A. Spruance, USN; Lieutenant General Holland M. Smith, USMC; Vice Admiral Richmond K. Turner, USN; Major General Thomas E. Watson, USMC; Major General Clifton B. Cates, USMC. (US Navy)

Above: Members of a US Marines' patrol remove a tiny girl from the debris of a shelter in which she and her father had been hiding for weeks on Tinian, circa August 1944.

Above: A lone member of the 24th Marines, 4th Marine Division patrols the streets of Tinian Town. Surrounded by the evidence of the bitter fighting in the area, he is passing a Shinto shrine. (USMC Archives)

Below: Post is handed out to a group of battle-weary US Marines on Tinian. (USMC Archives)

Chapter 9

MOPPING UP

3 August 1944–1 January 1945

Considerable numbers of Japanese were still at large on Tinian, and they still posed a threat to the Marines. As already mentioned, on 3 August, the 4th Division was attacked, an action in which forty-seven of the enemy were killed.

Below: A 75mm pack howitzer in action up on the position known as 'The Crow's Nest' on 25 August 1944. The Marines' gunners are using it to fire on Japanese troops holding out in a cave on one of the sheer cliff faces in the southern part of Tinian. The gun, nicknamed *Miss Connie*, had been lashed into place on this unusual and somewhat precarious spot after it had been dismantled, carried up the nearby slopes by hand and then reassembled in situ. (NARA)

More disturbing on that day, however, were incidents over which the Americans had no control. To the dismay and anguish of many of the Marines, they witnessed individual and collective suicides by the Japanese on the cliffs at Marpo Point. They saw Japanese children being thrown to their deaths into the ocean by their parents who then followed them over the edge; they saw Japanese military personnel gather groups of fifteen to twenty civilians and attach explosive charges to them before 'blowing them to bits'. Japanese troops and civilians lined up on the top of the cliffs to jump into the sea, and when civilians would not willingly fling themselves over the edge, they were simply pushed over by the military.[29]

In an effort to save as many lives and as much time as possible, General Cates ordered one of the most respected Japanese on the island, the manager of the largest sugar cane factory, to encourage the civilians to surrender. After persistent pleading, a woman and four children walked out into the open. They formed a circle, straightened their clothes, bowed to each other and then blew themselves up with grenades. This was followed immediately afterwards with a woman running to the edge of the cliff to throw her two children into the sea before jumping after them.[30]

Robert Sheeks, a USMC Language and Intelligence Officer who served on both Saipan and Tinian, later recalled the problems the Marines faced: 'There were many instances of suicide, and nearly every civilian, as well as every soldier, had been issued one or more grenades with instructions to save one for suicide at the end.'[31]

Seeing no alternative, the Marines issued an ultimatum on the afternoon of 3 August. Using public address systems, the Americans called out to the Japanese: 'Come out by 0830, 4 August, or caves will be blown up.'

This prompted thousands of civilians to emerge from their hideouts and surrender. Major General James L. Underhill, who had been appointed the island's military commander at the end of the invasion, described the state of these people: 'They came in with no possessions except the rags on their backs. They had been under a two-month intense bombardment and shelling and many were suffering from shell shock ... They had existed on very scant rations for six weeks and for the past week had had practically nothing to eat. They had been cut off from their own water supply for a week and had caught what rainwater they could in bowls and cans. Hundreds of them were wounded and some of their wounds were gangrenous.'[32] More than 9,000 Japanese civilians gave themselves up. Very few Japanese soldiers joined them.

This meant that the Marines were faced with an almost insurmountable job clearing the immense number of almost impenetrable caves. So, the fighting went on.

On 4 August, a battery of the 14th Marines attached to the Northern Troops Landing Force was attacked by fifteen Japanese in a cane field, with twelve of the latter being killed. That day was also marked by another action which resulted in the awarding of a second Medal of Honor for the fighting on Tinian.

Private First Class Robert Lee Wilson was serving in Company D, 2nd Pioneer Battalion, 18th Marines of the 2nd Marine Division. Wilson's citation provides the following detail: 'As one of a group of Marines advancing through heavy underbrush to neutralize isolated points of resistance, Private First Class Wilson daringly preceded his companions toward a pile of rocks where Japanese troops were supposed to be hiding. Fully aware of the danger involved, he was moving forward while the remainder of the squad, armed with automatic rifles, closed together in the rear when an enemy grenade landed in the midst of the group. Quick to act, Private First Class Wilson cried a warning to the men and unhesitatingly threw himself on the grenade, heroically sacrificing his own life that the others might live and fulfil [sic] their mission.'

Above: A US Marine hunts for Japanese snipers in the Tinian brush during July or August 1944. (USNHHC)

All together the capture of Tinian had cost the invading ground forces a total of 328 killed and 1,571 wounded in action, almost all of them Marine Corps personnel. Admiral Spruance called the island's capture, 'The most brilliantly conceived and executed operation in World War II'. General Holland Smith agreed, saying it was 'the perfect amphibious operation of the Pacific War'.

There were no such accolades for the Japanese. Of the 8,000-plus army and navy troops on the island, barely 252 had been taken prisoner by the end of operations in August. All the rest had either been killed or were simply never seen again.

From 6 August 1944, moves were undertaken to deploy the bulk of the Marines out of Tinian, leaving just the 8th Regiment to complete the mopping up. This dangerous and unpleasant task continued until 1 January 1945. In that time the number of Japanese killed totalled 542, but they inflicted 163 casualties on the 8th Marines, of whom thirty-eight were killed and 125 wounded.

Left: US Marines set off a dynamite charge to blow up a Japanese dugout to pieces on Tinian. 'Sailing high into the air on the left,' notes the original caption, 'is the helmet of a soldier who refused to surrender'. (National Museum of the US Navy)

Below: US Marine Sergeant Charles Monges gives a cup of water to a little Japanese girl who wandered out of the woods on Tinian, August 1944. (USNHHC)

Right: Personnel of Naval Construction Battalion No.121 are pictured installing a floating fuel pipeline off White beach, Tinian, on 25 October 1944. (USNHHC)

Above: Private First Class Robert L. Wilson, who hailed from Centralia, Illinois, was posthumously awarded the Medal of Honor for throwing himself on a hand grenade and sacrificing his own life in order to save the lives of fellow Marines on Tinian. (NARA)

Left: The end of the battle on Tinian is in sight as the mopping operations enter their final stages. Here a US Marine looks down from a cliff top as his comrades, and more specifically men of the 24th Marines and the 4th Tank Battalion, comb across the scrub at the island's extreme southern tip. The 23rd Marines, whose area ended at the top of the steep cliff seen here, had to retrace their steps in order to reach the lowlands. The outline of Aguijan Island can be seen in the distance. (NARA)

Below: A captured Japanese 6-inch coastal defence gun pictured after its capture on Tinian, circa August 1944. (National Museum of the US Navy)

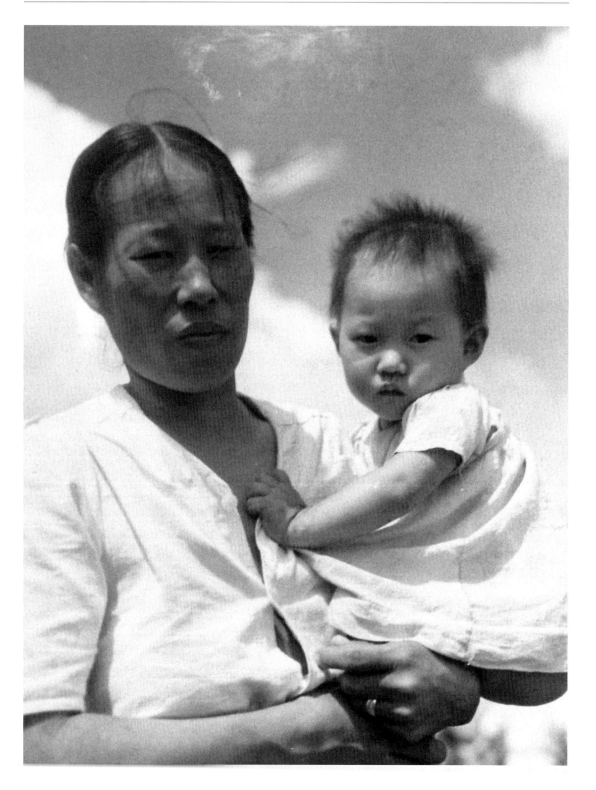

Left: A Japanese mother and her child pictured while being held in Camp Churo on Tinian in June or July 1945. Following the capture of Tinian, the US military authorities established Camp Churo to care for, as well as bring some semblance of organization, to Tinian's 10,635 non-military inhabitants. This camp was actually misnamed, the original intention being to call it Camp Chulu, within which Tinian village it was built. The site was chosen by virtue of the water wells that existed in the area, it being felt that these would best serve the needs of the civilians. The camp was divided into two sections. One held some 8,278 Japanese and Okinawan civilians, the second was used to house some 2,357 Koreans who had been brought in by the Japanese to work in the sugarcane fields. (National Museum of the US Navy)

Below: A veteran of the landings on Roi-Namur and Saipan, Marine Corps Combat Correspondent Staff Sergeant Federico Claveria, serving with the 5th Amphibious Corps, gives an interned Tinian child some sweets, August 1944. This is possibly another shot taken at Camp Churo. (USMC Archives)

Above: Two US Marine Generals, Major General Harry Schmidt (left) and Major General Clifton B. Cates (centre), confer with Rear Admiral W. Chambers USN, the Inspector Medical Department Activities, Pacific Area, on Tinian in early August 1944. At the time, Chambers was undertaking an inspection of the medical facilities on the island. (National Museum of the US Navy)

Below: Japanese internees at Camp Churo, July 1945. There were 3,000 children in Camp Churo at its peak. Its inhabitants were repatriated to their respective homelands in 1946. (National Museum of the US Navy)

Chapter 10

TINIAN'S SECRET MISSION TRAGEDY

30 July 1945

She stretched for more than 600 feet and weighed in excess of 10,000 tons. The USS *Indianapolis* was one of just two Portland-class heavy cruisers which had been commissioned into the US Navy on 15 November 1932. It became the flagship of the US Navy's Scouting Force in 1933 and, as ship of state, carried President Franklin D. Roosevelt on multiple journeys. In the Second World War, USS *Indianapolis* had operated in the New Guinea and Aleutian campaigns and, in 1943, as flagship of Vice Admiral Raymond A. Spruance, commanding the Fifth Fleet. Her 8-inch main guns had shelled enemy positions during the recapture of Tarawa, as they had during the US conquest of the Marshall Islands. Further operations saw *Indianapolis* involved in attacking the Palau Islands before the start of Operation *Forager*.

As Spruance's flagship, *Indianapolis* took part in the Battle of the Philippine Sea before returning with the Fifth Fleet to continue the bombardment of Saipan on 23 June 1944. Six days later, she moved to Tinian to attack installations on the island ahead of the more targeted pre-invasion bombardment.

Below: USS *Indianapolis* anchored off the Mare Island Navy Yard, California, on 10 July 1945, after her final overhaul. Within days she would be underway to the island of Tinian loaded with her historic cargo. (NARA)

Left: Taken circa 26 July 1945, this picture shows the USS *Indianapolis*, in the centre distance, anchored off Tinian having just delivered the atomic bomb materials. This view was taken looking south from the south end of Tinian, with Aguijan Island in the background. (USNHHC)

When Guam was taken, *Indianapolis* became the first US ship to enter Apra Harbor since the Japanese occupation. The cruiser remained in the Marianas until early September when she sailed once more for the Carolines and then Peleliu before returning to the Mare Island Naval Shipyard in California for refitting.

After her overhaul, *Indianapolis* saw action in support of the landings on Iwo Jima and Okinawa. During the latter operation, the cruiser was hit by a Japanese bomb which penetrated the hull and caused other damage, necessitating a return to Mare Island.

Following lengthy repairs and a further overhaul, *Indianapolis* was ready once more to go back to war. Firstly though, she had another task to perform. It was one of the utmost secrecy, as her captain, Charles B. McVay III, related in a subsequent interview:

'On about 12 July [1945], I got orders which indicated that we had to perform some special mission, so that we knew that we would not be able to take our usual refresher course on the West Coast, but had been told we would receive that in the forward area. On 15 July, I was in San Francisco, and talked with Admiral Purnell and Captain Parsons who I know were connected in an intimate way with a secret project, but I did not know what this project was. I was informed at that time that when we were ready for sea on 16 July, we would proceed as fast as possible to the forward area.'

At Hunter's Point Naval Dockyard, *Indianapolis* took onboard a number of items, including one crate that was to be taken to the Admiral's quarters, crewmembers being told that if anything should happen to *Indianapolis*

131

it had to be put on a lifeboat before anything else. In that crate were the 'gun-type' mechanism for the first ever atomic bomb, named *Little Boy*, and half of the supply of the bomb's uranium.

Naturally, rumours surrounding the ship's cargo spread like wildfire. 'Everyone was betting on what those crates contained,' one crewman remembered. 'One person said it contained bottles of whiskey for all the crew to celebrate the end of the war; another that it was a Cadillac for General MacArthur, and even that it contained 20,000 scented toilet rolls for that general. But, as the men later said, if they would have been told it was parts for the atomic bomb it would not have meant anything to them anyway as the *Indianapolis* was always loaded with shells and explosives.'[33]

USS *Indianapolis* sailed from San Francisco at 08.00 hours on the morning of 16 July. Speed had been demanded of her and the heavy cruiser set a record time of 74.5 hours to complete the passage from San Francisco to Pearl Harbor, achieving an average speed of twenty-nine knots. She arrived at Pearl Harbor on 19 July.

McVay had been told to arrive at Tinian on 26 July, a further 1,400 miles from Hawaii. He calculated that *Indianapolis* only needed to travel that distance at a steady 24 knots to be there at the required time. Encountering no problems, the cruiser reached Tinian on the morning of the 26th.

As soon as the secret cargo had been unloaded, McVay sailed without delay to Guam, which was reached around 10.00 hours the following day. After replenishing her stores and fuel, McVay was given a route and speed that he had to maintain unless he had to go faster if some unforeseen difficulty arose. The destination was Leyte in the Philippines, and the required speed was a moderate 15.7 knots per hour to enable him to reach there at 11.00 hours on Tuesday, 31 July. *Indianapolis* duly departed Guam at the prescribed speed, zigzagging as she sailed until nightfall when, presumably, such evasive precautions were considered unnecessary.

It was a few minutes after midnight on 30 July that disaster struck. 'I was thrown from my emergency cabin bunk on the bridge by a very violent explosion,' continued McVay, which was 'followed shortly thereafter by another explosion. I went to the bridge and noticed, in my emergency cabin and charthouse, that there was quite a bit of acrid white smoke. I couldn't see anything.

'I got out on the bridge. The same conditions existed out there. It was dark, it was this whitish smoke. I asked the Officer of the Deck [senior officer on duty] if he had had any reports. He said "No, Sir. I have lost all communications".' USS *Indianapolis* had been hit on her starboard side by two torpedoes, one in the bow and one amidships, fired by the Japanese submarine *I-58*.

Devoid of all electrical communications, McVay went back to his cabin to put on his shoes and some clothes, in the process bumping into the damage control officer. The latter had gone down to assess the damage immediately after the first torpedo had struck. Lieutenant Commander Casey Moore told his captain that the cruiser was 'going down rapidly by the head'. He asked McVay if he should pass on the word to abandon ship.

McVay told him 'No'. The ship had only a slight list and it was not the first time that *Indianapolis* had been holed. However, just two or three minutes later, the executive officer, Commander Flynn, went up to McVay to report: 'We are definitely going down and I suggest that we abandon ship.' McVay bowed to the inevitable and the order was given to abandon *Indianapolis*.

Tragic though the order to abandon ship was, the cruiser was travelling between two US-held islands on a standard route (indeed she had overtaken LST *779* a few hours earlier on the afternoon

Left: USS *Indianapolis* alongside at the Mare Island Navy Yard on 12 July 1945. This was the day that Captain Charles B. McVay III received the orders for his ship's 'special mission'. (USNHHC)

Above: Another view of USS *Indianapolis* taken on 10 July 1945, this time bow-on. *Indianapolis* has been described as the last major US Navy ship sunk in the Second World War. (NARA)

Right: USS *Indianapolis* pictured during its earlier involvement with the Mariana Islands. Here the Portland-class heavy cruiser is under fire from Japanese shore batteries during the invasion of Saipan in June 1944. (USNHHC)

of the 29th on a similar passage to the Philippines) and it should not have been long before its absence was noted. The track of vessels in and out of Guam and Leyte were recorded on plotting boards except for large warships like *Indianapolis* which, unless either station was informed that there was a problem, were not monitored.

That, though, should not have been an issue, as a distress call was put out by *Indianapolis'* crew before the ship was abandoned. Three US stations received the signal, but unfortunately none acted upon the information. It is said that at these stations one commander was drunk, another had ordered his men not to disturb him, and a third thought it was a Japanese trap.[34]

Above: USS *Indianapolis* pictured while preparing to leave Tinian after delivering the atomic bomb components. (USNHHC)

Right: Lieutenant Wilbur C. Gwinn USNR was the pilot of the Ventura patrol bomber which first sighted the survivors of USS *Indianapolis* in the Philippine Sea on 2 August 1945. That day he was on the outward leg of his patrol when the weight fell from the navigational antenna trailing behind his aircraft. While crawling back through the fuselage to repair the thrashing antenna, Gwinn happened to glance down at the sea and noticed a long oil slick. Back in the cockpit, Gwinn dropped down to investigate.

At 11.20 hours, the crew spotted thirty survivors in the water. The plane's crew immediately dropped a life raft and a sonobuoy, before transmitting reports of their sighting. Gwinn continued to examine the oil slick, which ran in a north-easterly direction from the position of the first sighting. Another group of some 150 survivors was then found.

At 15.30 hours that afternoon, Lieutenant R. Adrian Marks, flying a PBY Catalina, was the first to arrive on the scene having been alerted by Gwinn's reports. Horrified at the sight of sharks attacking men below him, Marks, ignoring standing orders, landed his flying boat on the twelve-foot swell.

His crew, pulling a survivor aboard, became the first to learn the true facts of the *Indianapolis* disaster. Further men were pulled aboard, but space in the flying boat was limited, so Marks had some of the survivors lashed to the wing with parachute cord. This, however, damaged the wings and rendered the Catalina unflyable. It was not until nightfall that the destroyer USS *Cecil J. Doyle*, the first of seven rescue ships, reached the scene. It recovered the crew and sailors from the flying boat, which, unable to be recovered, was sunk. All told, Marks and his crew rescued fifty-six survivors. For his actions, Marks was awarded the Air Medal. (NARA)

Right: Ambulances lined up at Guam awaiting the arrival of USS *Tranquillity* with survivors of the sunken *Indianapolis*, 8 August 1944. Note the construction supplies in foreground, and ships beyond. (NARA)

Indianapolis sank in just twelve minutes, 280 miles from the nearest land. So, as the crew of USS *Indianapolis* abandoned ship into the dangerous waters of the largest ocean in the world, expecting to soon be rescued, daily operations continued in the Pacific as if nothing had happened.

The stories told by the survivors of the sinking are almost too harrowing to relate, but it is only through their words that a true understanding of the tragedy which befell the crew of *Indianapolis* can in some measure be appreciated. As they drifted with the currents and the winds, the crew became spread over a large area of sea. The first few hours passed without too much anguish, the men full of hope and expectation that rescue vessels would soon be seen over the horizon. No ships appeared – but sharks did.

'All the time, the sharks never let up,' remembered Boatswain's Mate Second Class Eugene Morgan. 'We had a cargo net that had Styrofoam things attached to keep it afloat. There were about 15 sailors on this, and suddenly, 10 sharks hit it and there was nothing left. This went on and on and on.'

Machinist's Mate Second Class Granville Crane recalled that, 'men began drinking salt water so much that they were very delirious. In fact, a lot of them had weapons like knives, and they'd be so crazy, that they'd be fighting amongst themselves and killing one another. And then there'd be others that drank so much [salt water] that they were seeing things. They'd say, "The Indy is down below, and they're giving out fresh water and food in the galley!" And they'd swim down, and a shark would get them. And you could see the sharks eating your comrade.'[35]

Left: The hospital ship USS *Tranquillity* arrives at Guam, carrying survivors of the heavy cruiser USS *Indianapolis*, on 8 August 1945. The bow of the destroyer escort USS *Steele* is visible in the foreground. (USNHHC)

The sharks were something John 'Jack' Hinken never forgot: 'Once in a while, someone would see a fin out there in the water and holler. Then we'd kick and beat the water hard to try to scare them off.' Sometimes 'they must have come swimming underneath, seen a leg hanging down in the water and just taken a bite. I remember one guy had the calf of his leg bitten out. He didn't live long.'[36]

It was only a chance sighting by a patrolling aircraft that saved the remaining surviving men. The rescue operation finally began on the very day that *Indianapolis* should have been safely berthed at Leyte.

Only 316 men of the almost 900 who took to the water when *Indianapolis* went down survived; two of those later died. It has been calculated that the *Indianapolis*' disaster resulted in the most shark attacks on humans in history. Having completed its Tinian mission, the sinking of the heavy cruiser was, and remains, the worst disaster ever recorded in the annals of the US Navy.

142

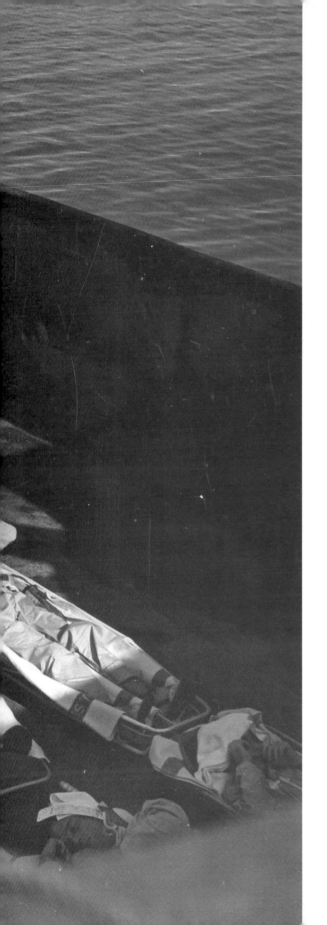

Above: Survivors from USS *Indianapolis* brought ashore from USS *Tranquillity* at Guam, 8 August 1945. They are being transferred by ambulances to local hospitals. (USNHHC)

Left: A landing craft transports injured survivors from USS *Indianapolis* ashore for hospitalization on Peleliu. (National Museum of the US Navy)

Below: The unloading of survivors from USS *Indianapolis* continues in Guam, circa 8 August 1945. (National Museum of the US Navy)

Above: Admiral Raymond Spruance, Commander US Fifth Fleet, awards a Purple Heart to RM1c Joseph Moran and two fellow survivors of the loss of USS *Indianapolis* at a base hospital on Guam. The picture is believed to have been taken on 13 August 1945. The other two men pictured are BGM3c Glenn Morgan (left) and S1c Louis Bitonti (right). Because many survivors were initially taken to Samar and Peleliu, they did not know the fate of all of their shipmates until they were all finally consolidated on Guam. (US Navy)

Right: S2/c Joseph A. Jacouemot, on the left, and S2/c Richard P. Thelen pictured recovering in hospital on Peleliu shortly after their rescue. 'I was sleeping when it [*Indianapolis*] blew up,' Thelen recalled in an interview he gave in 2019. 'I went flying in the air, but I don't know if I went 2 feet or 20 feet. I was covered with oil and twice, a shark came up and poked me with his nose in my life jacket. Sharks don't like the smell of diesel fuel and I was saturated in it. The diesel fuel saved my life.' Thelen, along with 95 fellow survivors, was picked up by the USS *Doyle* early in the morning of 3 August. At that point, he was too weak to climb a rope ladder to reach the ship. (NARA)

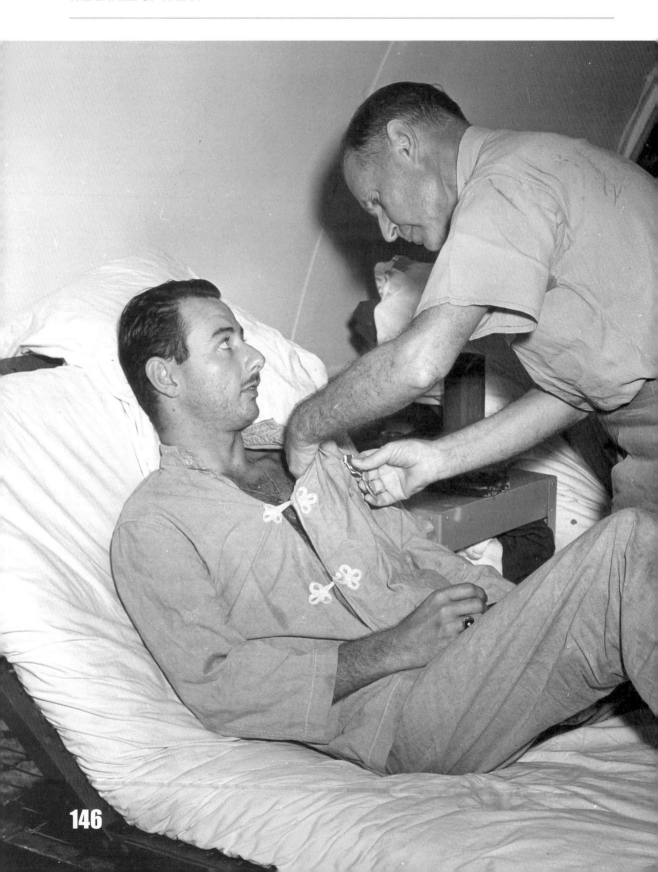

Left: Another *Indianapolis* survivor is decorated with the Purple Heart by Admiral Spruance at Guam on 13 August 1945. In this case, the individual is S1c Clarence E. McElroy, who sustained badly burned legs during the ship's sinking. (US Navy)

Above: Some of those who survived the sinking of USS *Indianapolis* are pictured in a hospital on Peleliu prior to 15 August 1945, on which date this picture was released to the press. (National Museum of the US Navy)

Right: The body of a member of USS *Indianapolis*' crew 'is borne to his lasting place' by survivors of the cruiser's sinking, August 1945. (NARA)

Below: Captain Charles B. McVay III speaks to a group of war correspondents regarding the sinking of USS *Indianapolis* on or before 15 August 1945. (National Museum of the US Navy)

Above: The Japanese submarine *I-58* photographed at Sasebo, Japan, on 28 January 1946. The sinking of USS *Indianapolis* was the submarine's only significant success during the Second World War. *I-58* was scuttled by the US Navy on 1 April 1946. (USNHHC)

Below: Also taken at Sasebo, Japan, on 28 January 1946, this picture shows the forward torpedo room on *I-58*. Behind the crew members are 21-inch torpedo tubes. (USNHHC)

Chapter 11

ATOMIC BOMB ISLAND

Even as the battle for Tinian was still raging, US Navy Construction Battalions, the Seebees, were hard at work repairing and then developing the airfield at Ushi Point to accommodate the largest military aircraft then in service – the Boeing B-29 Superfortress. The Seebees also built an air-conditioned bomb assembly building for an undisclosed top-secret mission, bomb loading pits and a dock large enough to accommodate the USS *Indianapolis*. In total, six airstrips were constructed on the island, in the process of which some eight million tons of earth moved or reshaped.[37]

At Ushi Point airfield, renamed North Field, the existing 4,380 feet runway was increased to 8,500 feet. A further three runways were built, making it the largest airfield in the world, eventually also becoming the busiest with aircraft taking off every minute of every day. Two more runways were built on Tinian at what was named West Field.

The airfields on the Mariana Islands came under the auspices of XXI Bomber Command of the Twentieth Air Force, the latter having been brought into existence solely to conduct attacks upon

Below: As soon as the military situation following the US landings allowed it, work began on constructing new or improving existing former Japanese runways on Tinian. Here a Seebee unit is building an ancillary roadway. (NARA)

Right: Superfortresses of the Tinian-based B-29 fleet sweeping low over Seabees working on unfinished sections of the new Marianas airbase. Note the 'heavy 21-ton cat-and-earth mover' in the foreground being operated by Private Clarence Swinney. (National Museum of the US Navy)

Japan. To North Field flew the 313rd Bombardment Wing, with the 58th Wing taking over West Field. Both wings were equipped with B-29s.

The initial missions undertaken by the Superfortresses were against Iwo Jima, the Truk Islands, and other Japanese-held areas. On 29 November 1944, the first direct mission against Japan flown from the Marians struck Tokyo. Later, they flew low-level night incendiary raids on area targets in Japan and supported the invasion of Okinawa by bombing Japanese airfields used by kamikaze pilots.

From March 1945, the USAAF began a series of fire-bomb attacks. The first of these took place on the night of 9/10 March, when a total of 346 B-29s left the airfields on the Marianas to carry out what would prove to be the single most destructive air raid of the Second World War so far. The Superfortresses dropped 1,665 tons of bombs which caused a massive firestorm which wiped-out 16 square miles of Tokyo, killing more than 80,000 people with more than 1 million Japanese losing their homes. The value of the Marianas, Tinian included, to the Allied war effort had become clear to all, as Japanese city after city was subjected to similar attacks.

Scientist Philip Morrison, who had been involved in the nuclear weapons programme since January 1943, described Tinian during the peak of its use by the USAAF: 'Tinian is a miracle. Here, 6,000 miles from San Francisco, the United States armed forces have built the largest airport in the world. A great coral ridge was half-leveled [sic[to fill a rough plain, and to build six runways, each an excellent 10-lane

Above: An image that demonstrates the sheer scale of the United States' aerial superiority in the Pacific towards the end of the Second World War. Boeing B-29 Superfortresses of the 768th Bombardment Squadron, 462nd Bombardment Group, pictured on Tinian on 11 April 1945. (NARA)

Right: The accomodation and administration area at North Field, Tinian, in 1945. (Harry S. Truman Library & Museum)

highway, each almost two miles long. Beside these runways stood in long rows the great silvery airplanes. They were not by the dozen, but by the hundred. From the air this island, smaller than Manhattan, looked like a giant aircraft carrier, its deck loaded with bomber[s].'[38]

In May 1945, a new formation arrived at North Field in the shape of the 509th Composite Group. This unit, under the command of Lieutenant Colonel Paul W. Tibbets Jr., was formed at the beginning of September 1944 with one purpose in mind – the delivery of atomic bombs.

The 509th began operating combat missions on 30 June 1945. They continued dropping bombs on Japanese-controlled islands throughout July to practice radar and visual bombing procedures. They also undertook missions against Japan proper. In these raids they dropped what were called 'pumpkin' bombs. These were conventional aerial bombs developed by the team engaged in constructing the atomic weapons, under the cover name of the 'Manhattan Project'. They were close replicas of one of the nuclear bombs, the *Fat Man* plutonium bomb. They had the same ballistic and

Right: The wreckage of Japanese aircraft frame the view of this B-29 Superfortress as it takes off from Tinian bound for a target in the Japanese Home Islands. (NARA)

handling characteristics, but inside were non-nuclear conventional high explosives.

Because the round trip to Japan was close to 3,000 miles, all bombers that took off from the island had to be overloaded with fuel. This requirement made accidents on take-off a relatively common occurrence – a problem that planners of the atomic bomb had not anticipated. If an aircraft carrying a primed nuclear bomb crashed on take-off, the consequences could be catastrophic. As a result, it was decided to arm the bomb in flight.

That decision was taken on 4 August. It was on that same day that Tibbets informed his men of the precise nature of their mission. The next day, 5 August 1945, the lead aircraft of the group, nicknamed *Enola Gay*, manoeuvred over a bomb pit, was loaded and then taxied to North Field's Runway Able.

At 02.45 hours on 6 August this B-29 – piloted by Tibbets himself – took off from Tinian. Three other aircraft had already departed on what was named Special Mission 13. Their roles were to assess the weather en route and over the primary and secondary targets and relay the information back to the strike aircraft, *Enola Gay*. Along with *Enola Gay* were two observation 'planes and a strike spare aircraft, named *Top Secret*, in case any early problems were encountered by Tibbets and his crew. When *Enola Gay* passed the point of no return, *Top Secret* landed at Iwo Jima.

At 08.15 hours Japanese time, Tibbets' atomic bomb, *Little Boy*, was dropped on Hiroshima. It exploded a minute later. The nuclear age was born.

While waiting for a response to the subsequent Allied demand for Japan to

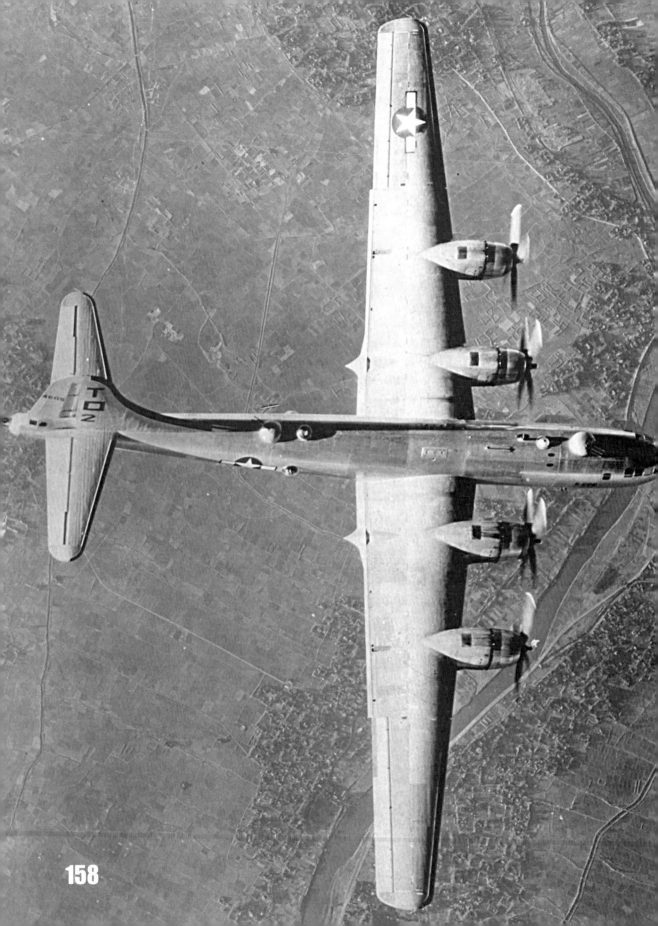

surrender, the Twentieth Air Force continued its attacks, including more operations by the 509th. Having received no reply from Tokyo, on 9 August, the B-29 *Bockscar*, loaded with the plutonium bomb *Fat Man*, lifted off from Runway Able.

Fat Man exploded over the city of Nagasaki at 11.02 hours local time. Emperor Hirohito announced Japan's unconditional surrender six days later.

Left: A B-29 Superfortress pictured whilst over the Tokyo district, more specifically the Tama River just west of the city. (NARA)

Below: A residential area of Tokyo that was destroyed during Operation *Meetinghouse* on the night of 9/10 March, 1945. (NARA)

Above: Three of the 509th Composite Group's Boeing B-29 Superfortress pictured before their mission to Hiroshima. From left to right they are *Big Stink*, *The Great Artiste*, and, nearest the camera, *Enola Gay*. (Courtesy of Harold Agnew)

Left: B-29 Superfortresses of the 21st Bomber Command, just visible centre right, fly over a memorial to the Taga people, prehistoric dwellers on Tinian, during January 1945. (NARA)

Below: An aerial view of North Field, Tinian, that was taken on 31 March 1945. It shows the four runways built for the B-29 Superfortresses. From right to left, these are Delta, Charlie, Baker and Able. (NARA)

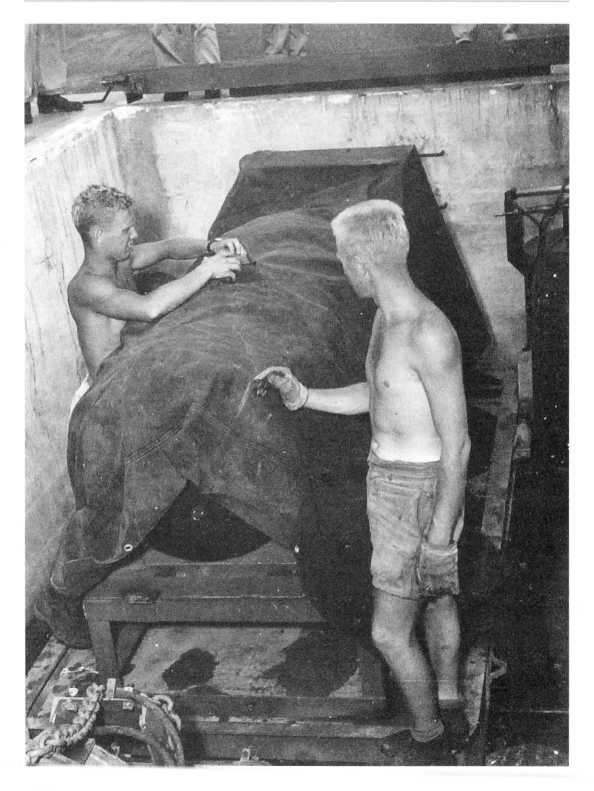

Above: A view of No.1 Bomb Loading Pit at North Field, Tinian, which is today covered by a protective roof. This was used to house *Little Boy*. (John Grehan Collection)

Left: A canvas cover is removed from *Little Boy* in No.1 Bomb Loading Pit on Tinian. The bomb weighed about 9,000lbs and had a yield equivalent to approximately 20,000 tons of high explosive. (National Museum of the US Navy)

Below: Bomb Loading Pit No.2, where *Fat Man* was stored and loaded onto *Bockscar*. *Fat Man* had to be armed before it was loaded into the B-29's bomb bay which meant that it was 'live' for the entire flight and once airborne the bomb could not be brought back. (John Grehan Collection)

Above: *Fat Man* on its transport carriage on Tinian Island following its final assembly in preparation for its use against Japan. In keeping with its name, *Fat Man* was more than twice as wide as *Little Boy* which was dropped on Hiroshima. (NARA)

Below: Runway Able, of North Field, Tinian, from where both *Enola Gay* and *Bockscar* lifted off on their historic flights to Hiroshima and Nagasaki. (John Grehan Collection)

Right: Colonel Paul W. Tibbets Jr., the commander of the 509th Composite Group, and pilot of *Enola Gay*, waves from his cockpit just moments before taking off from Tinian for the flight to Hiroshima on 6 August 1945. (NARA)

Above: One of the USAAF's 509th Composite Group's B-29s pictured in the air. Note the temporary triangle 'N' tail marking indicating that the aircraft is carrying a nuclear weapon. (National Museum of the US Air Force)

Right: Found archived away in an elementary school in Honkawa in 2013, this picture is believed to show the mushroom cloud over Hiroshima some thirty minutes after detonation of *Little Boy*, as seen from a location about 6 miles east of the hypocentre. (Honkawa Elementary School)

Overleaf: A Japanese soldier walks through the atomic bomb levelled city of Hiroshima in September 1945. (USNHHC)

Left: The mushroom cloud grows over Nagasaki, rising some 60,000 feet into the air, after *Fat Man* was dropped and exploded on 9 August 1945. (NARA)

Above: The destruction of Nagasaki as it appeared in September 1945. This view is of the area very close to ground zero. *Fat Man* exploded above Nagasaki's industrial valley – roughly halfway between the Mitsubishi Steel and Arms Works in the south and the Mitsubishi-Urakami Ordnance Works (a torpedo factory) in the north. This was nearly two miles north-west of the intended hypocentre. About one-third of Nagasaki City was destroyed in the explosion and 150,000 people were killed or injured. It was reputedly said at the time that the area would be devoid of vegetation for seventy-five years. (USNHHC)

Above: Lieutenant Commander Edward Porter Clayton, USN, who can be seen in the centre with his back to the camera, the Commanding Officer of Underwater Demolition Team 21, receives the first sword surrendered to an American force in the Japanese Home islands. The surrender was made by a Japanese Army Coast Artillery Major at Futtsu-misaki Navy Base, on 28 August 1945. (USNHHC)

Overleaf: Pictured from atop USS *Missouri*'s 16-inch No.2 gun turret the battleship anchored in Tokyo Bay, General Yoshijiro Umezu signs the Instrument of Surrender on behalf of Japanese Imperial General Head-quarters, 2 September 1945. This was the moment that the Second World War finally came to an end. (NARA)

NOTES AND REFERENCES

1   Samuel Eliot Morison, *History of United States Naval Operations in World War II, Vol. 8: New Guinea and the Marianas, March 1944 to August 1944* (Little, Brown & Co., Boston, 1953), p. 233.

2   Commander David Moore USN (Retd.), *The Battle of Saipan - The Final Curtain*, www.battleofsaipan.com

3   Victor Brooks, *Hell is Upon Us, D-Day in the Pacific, June-August 1944* (Da Capo Press, Cambridge, 2005), pp.221-2.

4   Derrick Wright, *Pacific Victory, Tarawa to Okinawa 1943-1945* (Sutton, Stroud, 2005), p.90.

5   Major Carl W. Hoffman, *The Seizure of Tinian* (USMC Historical Monograph), p.16.

6   ibid, p.27.

7   For further information on the operations regarding this island, see John Grehan and Alexander Nicoll, *Saipan 1944: The Most Decisive Battle of the Pacific War* (Frontline Books, Barnsley, 2021).

8   Peculiarly, while the US Army (and the British) referred to these as Landing Vehicle, Tracked, the US Marines referred to them as Amphibious Vehicle, Tracked, the 'L' being used to denote amphibious vessels.

9   Richard Harwood, *A Close Encounter: The Marine Landing on Tinian* (Marine Corps Historical Center, Washington D.C., 1994), p.6.

10   ibid, p.4.

11   Nathan N. Prefer, *The Battle for Tinian. Vital Stepping Stone in America's War Against Japan* (Casemate, Oxford, 2012), pp.77-8.

12   ibid, pp.73-4.

13   ibid, p.76.

14   Philip A. Crowl, *United States Army in World War II, The War in the Pacific, Campaign in the Marianas* (Center of Military History, United States Army, Washington, 1993), p.293.

15   *Handbook on Japanese Military Forces*, Chapter. VII, Japanese Tactics, 1 June 1945, p.2.

16   Quoted from 'Marine Fight For Tinian', warfarehistorynetwork.com.

17   Richard Harwood, *A Close Encounter: The Marine Landing on Tinian* (Marine Corps Association, 1994), p.10.

18 Carl W. Proehl, *The Fourth Marine Division in World War II* (Infantry Journal Press, Washington,1946), p.101.

19 Quoted in Hoffman, p.66.

20 Harwood, p.6.

21 Prefer, pp.119-120.

22 Letter by Lieutenant Colonel Walter F. Layer dated 16 November 1950, quoted in Hoffman, p.99.

23 Harwood, p.25.

24 ibid, pp.24-5.

25 Hoffman, p.112,

26 ibid, p.117.

27 Henry I. Shaw, Jr. and Bernard C. Nalty, *History of U.S. Marine Corps Operations in World War II*, Volume III: Central Pacific Drive (Historical Branch, G-3 Division, Headquarters, U.S. Marine Corps, 1966), p.421.

28 ibid, p.422.

29 Harwood, p.29.

30 Prefer, p.155.

31 Alexander Astroth, *Mass Suicides on Saipan and Tinian*, 1944 (McFarland, Jefferson, 1992), p.106.

32 Harwood, p.12.

33 *Indianapolis: The Legacy* 2015 film directed by Sara Vladic.

34 Timothy W. Maier, 'For The Good of the Navy', *Insight on the News*, 5 June 2000.

35 See: www.history.com/news/uss-indianapolis-sinking-survivor-stories-sharks

36 *Norfolk Daily News*, 2 September 2017.

37 Prefer, p.163.

38 Richard Rhodes, *The Making of the Atomic Bombs* (Simon and Schuster, New York, 1986), p.681.

SELECTED BIBLIOGRAPHY

Crowl, Philip A., *United States Army in World War II, The War in the Pacific, Campaign in the Marianas* (Center of Military History, United States Army, Washington D.C., 1993)

Harwood, Richard, *A Close Encounter: The Marine Landing on Tinian* (Marines in World War II Commemorative Series)

Hoffman, Major Carl W., *The Seizure of Tinian* (USMC Historical Monograph Historical Branch, G-3 Division, Headquarters, U.S. Marine Corps, 1951)

Maier, Timothy W., 'For The Good of the Navy'. *Insight on the News*, 5 June 2000.

Morison, Samuel Eliot *History of United States Naval Operations in World War* II, *Vol. 8: New Guinea and the Marianas, March 1944 to August 1944* (Little, Brown & Co., Boston, 1953)

Prefer, Nathan N. *The Battle for Tinian. Vital Stepping Stone in America's War Against Japan* (Casemate, Oxford, 2012)

Rhodes, Richard, *The Making of the Atomic Bombs* (Simon and Schuster, New York, 1986)

Rottman, Gordon L., *Saipan & Tinian 1944: Piercing the Japanese Empire* (Osprey, Oxford, 2004)

Toland, John, *The Rising Sun, The Decline and Fall of the Japanese Empire 1936–1945* (Pen & Sword, Barnsley, 2011)